THE REAL AMERICAN DREAM

THE WILLIAM E. MASSEY SR. LECTURES IN THE

HISTORY OF AMERICAN CIVILIZATION

1998

D1216279

THE REAL AMERICAN DREAM

A Meditation on Hope

ANDREW DELBANCO

HARVARD UNIVERSITY PRESS

CAMBRIDGE, MASSACHUSETTS

LONDON, ENGLAND

First Harvard University Press paperback edition, 2000

Designed by Gwen Nefsky Frankfeldt

LIBRARY OF CONGRESS CATALOGING-IN-PUBLICATION DATA

Delbanco, Andrew, 1952–
The real American dream: a meditation on hope /
Andrew Delbanco.
p.   cm. — (The William E. Massey, Sr. lectures
in the history of American civilization ; 1998)
Includes bibliographical references and index.
ISBN 0-674-74925-1 (cloth)
ISBN 0-674-00383-7 (pbk.)
1. United States—Civilization—Philosophy.
2. National characteristics, American.
3. Melancholy—Social aspects—United States—History.
4. Puritans. 5. Nationalism—United States—History.
6. Self—Social aspects—United States—History—20th century.
I. Title. II. Series.
E169.1.D416 1999
973'.01—dc21   99-21179

TO ALAN HEIMERT

Perhaps in the first years of his teaching he felt as a military
man might feel when obliged to read the prayers at a fu-
neral. He probably conceived what he said more deeply than
a more scholastic mind might have conceived it; yet he
would have been more comfortable if someone else had said
it for him. I think he was glad when the bell rang, and he
could be himself again until the next day. But in the midst
of this routine of the class-room the spirit would sometimes
come upon him, and leaning his head on his hand, he would
let fall golden words, picturesque, fresh from the heart, full
of the knowledge of good and evil.

GEORGE SANTAYANA ON
WILLIAM JAMES

ACKNOWLEDGMENTS

WARM THANKS are due to Professor Werner Sollors, chair of the program in the History of American Civilization at Harvard, and to his colleagues, for their kind attentiveness during my week in Cambridge. I was honored by the invitation to deliver the William E. Massey Sr. Lectures, and touched by the many friends, teachers, and former colleagues who made the effort—some from afar—to attend. Christine McFadden, administrator of the program, was graciously accommodating at every turn, and made my stay uneventful in the best sense. It was a particular pleasure to talk, over a long lunch, with a group of graduate students whose striking combination of ingenuousness and professionalism greatly encouraged me about the future of our field.

Acknowledgments

The lectures are published here substantially as they were delivered, and I have not tried to disguise their original form as a composition to be spoken. Yet I have been conscious of differences between the word heard and the word read, and I owe thanks to Aida Donald and Camille Smith at Harvard University Press for their patience while I made revisions with those differences in mind. As always, my wife, Dawn, gave me criticism and encouragement when each was needed. For these generosities, and for incalculably more, I thank her.

CONTENTS

Prologue   1

1   GOD   13

2   NATION   45

3   SELF   81

Notes   121

Index   139

THE REAL
AMERICAN DREAM

Prologue

THE premise of this book is that human beings need to organize the inchoate sensations amid which we pass our days—pain, desire, pleasure, fear—into a story. When that story leads somewhere and thereby helps us navigate through life to its inevitable terminus in death, it gives us hope. And if such a sustaining narrative establishes itself over time in the minds of a substantial number of people, we call it culture. Without some such symbolic structure by which hope is expressed, one would be, as the anthropologist Clifford Geertz has put it, "a kind of formless monster with neither sense of direction nor power of self-control, a chaos of spasmodic impulses and vague emotions." We must imagine some end to life that transcends our own tiny allotment of days and hours if we are to keep at bay the "dim, back-of-the-mind suspicion that one may be adrift in an absurd world."[1]

The name for that suspicion—for the absence or diminution of hope—is melancholy. Melancholy is the dark twin of hope. Ever since it acquired a name from the Greek words for black bile, *melanos chole*, it has been thought to exert a particularly strong hold on certain people, and, as the great anatomist of melancholy Robert Burton put it, to afflict certain "kingdoms, provinces, and Politickal Bodies [that] are subject in like manner to this disease." As for what accounts for it, it has been attributed to too much gall and too little serotonin; and it has been treated by everything from a dose of scripture (which in the seventeenth century was called "that physic [that] works most kindly [by making] the party sick before it works") to the sunlamp cure for what we nowadays call Seasonal Affective Disorder, or S.A.D.[2]

The first to elaborate a theory of melancholy in its particular American form—of how it shadows the hopeful promise of our exuberant democracy—was not an American writer, but a visiting Frenchman, Alexis de Tocqueville. "Among democratic nations," Tocqueville wrote after his tour of the United States in the 1830s,

> men easily attain a certain equality of condition, but they can never attain as much as they desire. It per-

petually retires from before them, yet without hiding itself from their sight, and in retiring draws them on. At every moment they think they are about to grasp it; it escapes at every moment from their hold. They are near enough to see its charms, but too far off to enjoy them; and before they have fully tasted its delights, they die.

That is the reason for the strange melancholy that haunts inhabitants of democratic countries in the midst of abundance.[3]

Tocqueville thought that envy and longing were built into American life: that Americans suffered from the illusion that equality could eradicate their envy and prosperity could quench their yearning for happiness. These were illusory hopes, he believed, because "the incomplete joys of this world will never satisfy [the human] heart."[4]

Any history of hope in America must, therefore, make room at its center for this dogged companion of hope—the lurking suspicion that all our getting and spending amounts to nothing more than fidgeting while we wait for death. When I say "center," I mean it in the gravitational sense of the word—the point around which we orbit, and toward which, if we lose velocity, we fall. This idea is contained not only in certain theological and psychological doctrines, but in the colloquial terms with which we speak about the *experience* of melancholy: we sink, droop, break down.

3

Even the etymology of our modern word, depression—
from the Latin, *de primere*, to press down—contains this
idea of a fall.

At least since the Puritan poet Michael Wigglesworth reported in the 1650s that he felt "disrested" and
"sapless," a great many American writers have written
about this feeling of slack spirit and drift that we
sometimes call "marking time."[5] Mark Twain called it
the "fantods" (a term nicely glossed by the *Dictionary of
American Regional English* as "a fit of the sulks").
Melville called it the "hypos." In his great essay "Experience," Emerson gives a memorable description of
what it is like to be caught in a mid-life trance from
which one cannot be roused: "We wake and find ourselves on a stair, there are stairs below us, which we
seem to have ascended; there are stairs above us, many
a one, which go upward and out of sight. But . . . we
cannot shake off the lethargy now at noonday."[6]

A fundamental question of our literature has always
been how to find release from this feeling of living
without propulsion and without aim; and every writer
drawn to the theme has concluded, with the English
philosopher Michael Oakeshott, that hope depends on
finding some "end to be pursued more extensive than a
merely instant desire."[7] The history of that pursuit in
America is what I shall sketch in the pages that follow.
Let me summarize it briefly in advance.

In the first phase of our civilization, hope was chiefly

expressed through a Christian story that gave meaning to suffering and pleasure alike and promised deliverance from death. This story held the imagination largely without challenge for nearly two hundred years. In the second phase, as Christianity came under pressure from Enlightenment rationality, the promise of self-realization was transformed into the idea of citizenship in a sacred union. This process, which began before the Revolution and did not run its course until the 1960s, has been efficiently described by Conor Cruise O'Brien, who makes clear that it was by no means unique to the United States: "The Enlightenment removes a personal God . . . delegitimizes kingship, by desacralizing it," and substitutes "the people—a particular people in a particular land . . . the idea of a deified nation."[8] Finally, in the third phase— our own—the idea of transcendence has detached itself from any coherent symbology. It continues to be pursued through New Age spirituality, apocalyptic environmentalism, and the "multicultural" search for ancestral roots; but our most conspicuous symbols (to use a word considerably degraded since it appeared at the opening of the Gospel according to John) are the logos of corporate advertising—the golden arches and the Nike swoosh. Though vivid and ubiquitous, such symbols will never deliver the indispensable feeling that the world does not end at the borders of the self.

This is our contemporary dilemma: we live with

undiminished need, but without adequate means, for attaining what William James called the feeling of "elation and freedom" that comes only "when the outlines of the confining selfhood melt down."[9]

BEFORE I elaborate on this highly schematic account of what I take to be the three basic phases of American history, I want to say a few words about some of the methodological difficulties it raises. If we try to approach history, in R. G. Collingwood's phrase, by discovering "the outside of events," we shall never grasp something as elusive as the shape of hope or dread.[10] We shall never get hold of mental states by making inventories of numerable things. It is possible to chart the acceleration of locomotion and communications since the industrial age, the growing percentage of households with indoor plumbing and central heating since the Second World War, the jump in life expectancy since the discovery of antibiotics. But it is equally possible to graph rising rates of illegitimacy, divorce, juvenile crime, and the expanding disparity between the incomes of rich and poor. Such taunting symmetries are what Norman Mailer had in mind when he remarked that the problem in understanding even the recent past is that "history is interior."[11] Getting at the interior thought of a friend, or a spouse, or one's own child is hard enough; trying to catch the mood of strangers in the present, even with the help of pollsters, is harder. But retrieving something as fragile and fleeting as thought or feeling from the past is like trying to seize a bubble.

One reason it is hard is that most of the voices still audible to us come from a tiny minority who left written accounts of their experience; and the relation is often mysterious between these few and the many more whom time has rendered silent. What, for example, is one to make of Walt Whitman's comment that during the Civil War "the People, of *their own choice,* [were] fighting, dying for their *own* idea"? How could Whitman know this—and what, exactly, does it mean for a people to possess, or be possessed by, an idea? Who, indeed, *were* the people? And how do we place Whitman's remark in relation to the high rates of desertion in that war, or to the brutal draft riots that swept through New York City at its height, when white mobs pulled black men out of their homes for lynching, then dragged their bodies through the streets by the genitals? Was this really a war of, by, and for the people? Or was it a war between industrialists and slaveowners in which people were fodder?[12]

In the face of such obscurities, the best we can usually manage is to take the scraps left by witnesses and try to assemble them, as if they were fossil fragments, into a reconstructed skeleton. The result will always be incomplete, and we can only guess at the missing parts. Today, after the decline of positivism and the rise

7

of a pragmatist conception of truth as "any idea that helps us to *deal* . . . with . . . reality,"[13] we tend to acknowledge that the "truth" of what we reconstruct is a function of the quality of our guessing—and that the guess is limited by our preoccupations of the moment.

Let me say one more preliminary word about what might be called the civic dimension of the historian's task. It is a worthy goal to describe with fidelity and sympathy the stories human beings tell about their world in their effort to sustain themselves with hope; but the really difficult question is how to evaluate these stories. Can we make any judgments about whether they are good stories or bad?

One envies the scientists for having a ready answer to this question. They evaluate the stories they tell by testing experimentally how well those stories predict events in the material world. In the humanities, too, we try to measure our claims "scientifically" against what can be documented about the world—which is why, even in our mischievous "postmodern" mood, it would be an outrage against truth to say, for example, that there was no slavery in the antebellum United States. But once we shift the question and ask not whether but *why* there was slavery, we enter into an entirely different realm of storytelling, where the empirical standard gives us little help. The reference point for judgment becomes as much the unknowable future as the "known" past.

8

This is because our sense of the future changes according to whether we claim that slavery arose (as some of its practitioners asserted) because black people were culturally or biologically inferior, or because it was willed by God, or because it suited the cupidity and cruelty of white people, or because it emerged from African tribal rivalries, or because mercantile capitalism required it. In just the same way, it makes a difference how we answer the question of why slavery came to an end—of how hope, however meager, was restored to people to whom it had been denied. Did the Emancipation Proclamation, as Richard Hofstadter once described it, "have all the moral grandeur of a bill of lading"?[14] Or was it the culmination of a great moral struggle involving black people and white people alike?

Historians, as I have said, try to answer such questions in ways that are consistent with what is known about the past. But, as every teacher knows, we also owe something to the future. As I talk with my students, I can propose to them a "true" story about America that has at its center the poisonous idea of race. This story runs from Thomas Jefferson's obscene remark that the Orangutan prefers "black women over those of his own species," to W. E. B. Du Bois's experience a century later of coming face to face in a natural history museum with "a series of skeletons arranged from a little monkey to a tall well-developed white man, with a Negro barely outranking a chimpanzee."[15] But Jefferson and Du Bois can also be linked by a story about America's struggle to live up to the principle of inviolable rights that Jefferson wrote into the Declaration of Independence and that Du Bois spent his life defending and trying to enlarge. Both of these stories are true. Neither should be suppressed or allowed to supplant the other—because separately they impair the possibility of a collective future, whereas together they may help us achieve a future in which all Americans feel part of a culture that treats them with dignity and to which they owe respect. In this sense, the future is always at stake in how we understand the past.

In these introductory comments I have tried to clarify what I mean by some of the keywords I'll be using, such as *culture, melancholy,* and *hope.* I wish to make one last lexical remark, this time about the word *history.* Many philosophers, from Vico to Foucault, have proposed that history moves in a tidal rhythm by which a dominant idea exerts its force for a time, then falls away, to be succeeded by a new idea of comparable magnetic power. One of the best expressions of this way of thinking about the past—sometimes called idealism—comes from Emerson: "Our culture is the predominance of an idea which draws after it this train of cities and institutions. Let us rise into a new idea, and they will disappear."[16]

I shall now attempt to describe in sequence the three

ideas—God, nation, and . . . what? the market? the recreational self?—by which Americans have tried to save themselves from the melancholy that threatens all reflective beings. In a brief conclusion, I shall propose a few thoughts about what new idea, if any, may be gathering form and strength to succeed them as the old forms of hope pass away.

CHAPTER

1

GOD

L ET me begin by proposing to do something that the historian Alan Taylor has recently described as "quaint." "What could be more quaint," he asks, "than to seek [the roots of American identity] in colonial New England, the land of Puritans, Salem witches, the *Mayflower,* and Plymouth Rock?" Of course, he is right. Anyone who has been even half-awake in the last twenty years or so knows it is no longer safe to assume, as Tocqueville did, that there is "not an opinion, not a custom, not a law" that the New England origin of American civilization does not explain. Nevertheless, that is where I shall look for some clues to understanding our culture as it was first established and as it has since evolved.[1]

Why New England? Perry Miller once wrote that Virginia, no less than Massachusetts, found its "energizing propulsion" in religion. Miller insisted that Virginia's idea of itself as a trading colony "was conceived in the bed of religion," and that its publicly announced motives of evangelizing Indians and stopping the imperial designs of French and Spanish papists were more than disguises draped over the tobacco trade. But the fact remains, as a more recent historian, Jon Butler, has put it, that organized Christianity in the South went through a long "starving time" during the years of settlement, while New England's churches were, from the start, institutions of first and last resort for most of its people. Religion was hardly absent or trivial in the early South. But by comparison with New England, it was relatively dormant—until invigorated by the waves of evangelical revival that swept through virtually all the American colonies beginning in the eighteenth century.[2]

So I turn first to New England not because it was the whole story of early America, but because it was the place where the purest—or, if you prefer, most virulent—strain of the Christian story first took hold, and from which many variant strains were disseminated. If we regard New England in this way as a sample, and look at it under magnification with a pathologist's eye, I think we can get a view of the structure of the first American form of hope.

The people who brought to America this first animating idea (or, more accurately, who brought the idea that overwhelmed the native cultures they encountered here) are known to us by a name given to them by their enemies. Derided as "precisians" or "precisionists," they were regarded by many of their fellow Englishmen as fanatics who insisted that the Anglican Church had been corrupted with garish ceremonies and needed to return to precise conformity with the pure forms of worship established by Christ's apostles sixteen hundred years before they were born. Among the names by which these people were mocked, the one that stuck was "Puritans."[3]

As it turned out, their demand for church reform was nonnegotiable. It entailed a vision of small, autonomous churches (not in the sense of physical structures made of stone or wood, but in the sense of believers joined voluntarily together for worship) that was simply incompatible with a state church in which authority descended from a remote king, through the bishops he appointed, to the parish clergy who, as bottom-rung beneficiaries of a patronage system, were more inclined to please their earthly masters than to serve God. For Puritans, on the contrary, church authority *a*scended from the laity to a pastor whose theological training and eloquence in the pulpit qualified him to serve the congregation as "God's mouth to the people."[4] Thus Puritans were sometimes called "Congregationalists" or "Independents."

The most incisive critic of this upside-down theory

of church government, Archbishop Richard Hooker, concluded as early as the 1590s that their craving for purity made these people unfit to live "amongst men," but suited them well for life "in some wilderness by themselves."[5] Hooker turned out to be prescient. Under harassment by Anglican authorities in the early seventeenth century, a number of Puritan preachers migrated with several thousand of their followers to what they called (in a phrase that revealed their attitude toward the native peoples who already lived there) the "*vacant* wilderness" of the New World.

Ever since, there has been a good deal of speculation about why they went. Tocqueville thought "it was a purely intellectual craving that called them from the comforts of their former homes." But according to a less generous observer who lived in their own time, the real reason they left was their misanthropy: "A Puritan is such a one as loves God with all his soul, but hates his neighbour with all his heart." By the beginning of our own century, this view had become the prevailing one. According to D. H. Lawrence, they came "to get *away*"; and to his own rhetorical question "away from what?"—Lawrence replied, "in the long run, away from themselves." In an especially cruel assessment, William Carlos Williams called them "hard and little" people, as if they were the last pathetic droppings expelled from a depleted England.[6]

The questions I want to ask about these stony people

are, What kind of happiness were they able to conceive? What form did hope take in their imagination?

THERE IS a clue, I think, in a letter sent from Massachusetts in 1630 by John Winthrop, first Governor of the Bay Colony, to his wife, whom he had left behind—temporarily, he hoped—in England:

> I never fared better in my life, never slept better, never had more content of mind, which comes merely of the Lord's good hand, for we have not the like means of these comforts here which we had in England, but the Lord is all sufficient, blessed be his holy name, if he please, he can still uphold us in this estate, but if he shall see good to make us partakers with others in more Affliction, his will be done, he is our God, and may dispose of us as he sees good.[7]

Expressed in phrases drawn almost intact from the Lord's Prayer ("blessed be his . . . name," "his will be done"), here is the core of the Puritans' faith—their willing submission to the "all-sufficient" God of Genesis. The place to which they had come was a place of spiritual as well as physical exposure, where one could experience anew Adam's discovery (Gen. 3:8-11) that when he tried to conceal his nakedness from God, there was nowhere to hide. Compared to the English Babylon the Puritans had left behind, New England was a wilderness barren of worldly comforts. But it was suffused by God. The true wilderness, they insisted, was the land they had fled, where God had been lost in the pomp and glitter of a prideful church. Winthrop's letter to his wife is one of the first expressions in our literature of the idea that worldly goods imperil the soul by lulling it into self-love.

In this sense, the New England Puritans reveled in their nakedness. Probably with Genesis 3 in mind (or Job 23: "I cannot behold *him* . . . But he knoweth the way that I take"), one of their leading preachers warned, with relish, that God "seeth all the pranks of the adulterer in the darkest night." God was, moreover, a nasty prankster himself—having made human beings not only capable of, but desperate for, the sweet "content that the exercise of love carries with it in the natural body," and then set that body on a course of decay toward extinction. He gave to human beings an inclination to love their helpless children, whom he suspended over the pit of death—keeping some alive till adulthood, dropping others, apparently capriciously, before they could walk or speak.[8]

When this dark and glowering God chastised them for their "frowardness" (their word for the restive impudence of the self), Puritans turned their own fear into an occasion for aesthetic contemplation—as in the most infamous metaphor they ever conceived, of which we get a preview in a sermon preached by the first-generation minister Thomas Shepard in the 1630s ("thou hangest but by one rotten twined thread . . . over the flames of hell"), but which is best known in Jonathan Edwards's version delivered a hundred years later at Enfield, Massachusetts, on the theme of "Sinners in the Hands of an Angry God." Speaking in a monotone, staring impassively at the bell rope at the back of the meetinghouse, Edwards brought penitents into the aisle begging for mercy:

> O Sinner! . . . you hang by a slender thread, with the flames of divine wrath flashing about it, and ready every moment to singe it and burn it asunder . . . and you have . . . nothing to lay hold of to save yourself . . . nothing of your own, nothing that you have ever done, nothing that you can do, to induce God to spare you one moment.[9]

If God should decide to pluck you from the fire before the thread breaks, it would be for no reason other than his own inscrutable whim.

Long after Puritanism in any strict sense had become a garbled cultural memory in America, this God turned up in one of the haiku-sized limericks that Stephen Crane (who was descended from a line of what he called "the old ambling-nag, saddle-bag, exhorting kind" of preachers) was writing at the end of his life:

> A man said to the universe:
> "Sir, I exist!"
> "However," replied the universe,

"The fact has not created in me
"A sense of obligation."[10]

Allowing for the modern irony, this is what Edwards called the "principal hinge" of his religion, the doctrine that God brings to his relation with humanity no reward for good behavior. Reformation theologians called this discredited idea of *quid pro quo* the Covenant of Works, which, they said, had been broken by Adam's primal act of disobedience. When, for his own mysterious reasons, God later revealed to Abraham (in Genesis 15) that he had chosen the Jewish people to live again in a promised land according to his commandments (a choice that many Christians have read as foreshadowing their own salvation), he acted "without any respect unto any goodness in Abraham . . . for it is nothing that God seeth in Abraham, for which he doth reveal his justification to him."[11]

Here we arrive at one of the keywords of reformed Christianity: *justification.* Derived from the Latin verb *justificare*—to judge, to forgive, to vindicate—it took on a new meaning during the Renaissance from the new technology of printing. Bits of metal type could no more line themselves up into straight margins than Ezekiel's bones could dance. They were dead, inert—and the compositor had to tap them into alignment with his "justifying" stick. Here was the Puritan image

22

of man: ragged and disordered, out of harmony with his fellows and with himself, unless and until God acts to make him acceptable to his sight.

I HAVE said that I will use the word *culture* to mean the stories and symbols by which we try to hold back the melancholy suspicion that we live in a world without meaning. What we know of the culture of early New England suggests that most people believed that even the smallest events were evidence of the power and judgment of the God I have just described. Sometimes they called him by his Aristotelian names—First Mover and Final Cause—which expressed how he had set the world on its course and was carrying it toward its destiny, or *telos.* They had no notion of randomness or chance as we do today. "That which seems Chance to us," they believed, "is as a word of God acquainting us with his will." And they had no sense of persons being capable of making their own history. In human events God made himself visible by inhabiting the lives of saints and martyrs whom he "employs to be Patterns of *Holiness* and *Usefulness.*" God was visibly at work in nature, too—in every drought and plague, in every ray of sunlight and every storm. "I bless God," one Massachusetts man said a few months after the earthquake of 1727, for "his late providence the Earth-quake which made me have quick Apprehension of my own Sins and guilt."[12]

Reading and writing about this alien religion occupied me for quite a few years during my youth and early middle age—a religion according to which human beings are helpless creatures in a world that is an effusion of God's imagination. (If you doubt how alien it is, let me point out that the editors of *New York Magazine* now use the word "Calvinism" to mean a fashion trend initiated by the clothes designer Calvin Klein.)[13] But I do not think I really grasped until recently the meaning of the enormous disproportion this religion posited between the majesty of God and the puniness of man.

I began to understand it under surprising circumstances. While working a few years ago on an essay about Alcoholics Anonymous, I attended some AA meetings around the country. There I met some desperate, and remarkably eloquent, people who found themselves in the grip of an addiction (Puritans would have called it a sin) from which they had sworn a thousand times to free themselves, but which they had never really escaped. One Saturday morning in a New York church basement I was listening to a crisply dressed young man whose every word and gesture gave the impression of grievously wounded pride. He talked at length about his faultlessness and his determination to avenge himself upon the many people who had traduced him. While he was speaking, the man sitting next to me—a black man of about forty, in dreadlocks and shades—leaned over and whispered, "I used to feel that way too, before I achieved low self-esteem."

This was more than a good line. For me, it was the moment I understood in a new way the religion I had claimed to know something about. As the speaker bombarded us with phrases like "taking control of my life," "believing in myself," "toughing it out," the man beside me took refuge in the old Calvinist doctrine that pride is the enemy of hope. What he meant by his joke about self-esteem was that no one can save himself by dint of his own efforts. He thought the speaker was still lost—lost in himself, but without knowing it.

This is just what the Puritan divine Richard Sibbes had meant nearly four centuries earlier when he said that most "men are not lost enough in their own feeling for a Saviour." What Sibbes and my neighbor at the AA meeting were talking about was the simultaneous imperative to give *up* and give *way* to a force outside the self that has been waiting for the barricade of pride to be lowered. William James (an inspiration to one of the founders of AA, and a great explicator of religion) likens this experience to one we all recognize in ourselves, especially as we grow older. When you strain to remember a forgotten name, James points out, and find that the harder you work at it the more it seems "jammed," it is only if you "give up the effort" that "the lost name comes sauntering into your mind." This was his metaphoric restatement of what Sibbes intended when he preached that "a holy despaire in ourselves is the ground of true hope." From here it is a short trip—the twelfth step for AA, the twelfth sign in Edwards's inventory of the signs of grace—to the fundamental precept that the only salvation from "despair in ourselves" is service to others.[14]

When Puritans insisted in these terms that the self without God is utterly helpless and, indeed, pointless, they were not claiming to have discovered a new truth or a new God. What they did claim was that their God was the true God of Abraham and Augustine. He had been obscured, they thought, by pseudo-wizards in clerical garb who tried to fool people into thinking they could appease him by mumbling Latin incantations or by shaking the smoke of incense out of a silver censer. Against those "to whom the *Mass-Book* is dearer than the *Bible*,"[15] Puritans insisted there was no penitence, no offering, no genuflection, that could coax God into leniency, and *nothing,* to use Edwards's reiterated word, a person could do to impress him. And though they never presumed to know exactly when or where or how God would strike the heart with the saving knowledge of his omnipotence, they thought it was less likely to happen in a cathedral furnished with the props of human pride than in an unadorned meetinghouse where the central experience was not witnessing a "dumb-show" but listening to a plainspoken sermon. Theirs was a religion of the ear, not the eye.

When these people got to New England and set up churches of their own, "the average churchgoer," according to one scrupulous modern scholar, "listened to something like seven thousand sermons in a lifetime, totalling somewhere around fifteen thousand hours of concentrated listening."[16] What they were listening for was hope. It was from sermons that they learned to think of themselves as belonging to a lineage of the faithful whom God had taken under his protection—sometimes by collecting them in sanctuaries as he was doing in New England, other times by scattering them through the world so their enemies could never find them all and round them up: "If . . . the Papists aske, where was the Church visible, before *Luther?* The answer is, it was visible, not in open Congregations . . . but in sundry members of the Church, as sweet spices and flowers, growing here and there, whom the Popes and their Instruments, like wilde Boares sought to root out, and yet God preserveth them."[17]

Sermons, then, were history lessons. But most of all, they were intricate maps of the soul. What they offered was expert guidance on how to tell whether the stirrings in your own heart were grounds for hope that God had chosen *you* for mercy. In the course of this instruction, laypeople had to learn how to distinguish between true and false grace—between the real thing and the counterfeit version that taunts you by lifting you up only to drop you down lower than where you began. (This is very much the way one hears the effect of alcohol described at AA meetings.) These debates became particularly ferocious during revivals, when the fault lines within and between churches split open. Some doubted there could be what James was later to call "growth in holiness without a cataclysm"; others warned that sudden bursts of spiritual desire were like the involuntary engorgement and release of sexual pleasure—"like a lightning, which after a sudden flash leaveth [us] more in darkness." Some thought true grace might come in a flash; others thought it was more likely to come as "a confused kind of tumult and lumber of thoughts" in which the sinner grows gradually aware of the pettiness of his own resentments.[18] But whether it came suddenly or slowly, the process of growth in grace culminated in the recognition that without connectedness to others, the self is lost.

What I am describing was a seventeenth-century "talking cure." Puritans were incessant talkers. And the talk did not go in only one direction. Ministers held private conferences with members of their flock, and sometimes required them to give public professions of faith before the whole congregation. For certain people the therapy evidently did not work; and for some it may even have made things worse. We read of one Englishwoman of "nimble quick Sparrow-hawk eye"

28

(she seems to have suffered from what today we would call bipolar disease) who shook off her worried ministers "as a great Mastiff turnes off many small curres, laughing at them" in manic despair at her lost condition. There is no hint that this desperate woman doubted God's reality. What she doubted, eventually at the expense of her sanity, was her reality to God.[19]

From Winthrop's journal we learn of another woman who sank into "a sad melancholic distemper near to frenzy," and of a man who "fell into some trouble of mind, and in the night cried out, 'Art thou come, Lord Jesus?' and with that leaped out of his bed in his shirt, and breaking from his wife, leaped out at high window into the snow, and ran about seven miles off, and being traced in the snow, was found dead next morning." From the trail of footsteps by which they found him, it was possible to "perceive, that he had kneeled down to prayer in divers places" in the snow.[20]

The "soul-physicians" who ministered to such people were working with a model of the psyche that strikingly prefigured the one invented three centuries later by Freud. The road to recovery, they thought, was through the dark terrain of self-knowledge. First came fear of punishment at the hands of the parental lawgiver. Then the parent's authority was supposed to transfer itself to a voice within the self (what Freud was to call the superego) and to turn its anger inward (upon what he would call the id). "A man that commits . . .

murder," as one Elizabethan minister put it, or "fornication, adulterie, blasphemy, etc., albeit he doth so conceal that matter that no man living know it, yet . . . he hath a griping in his conscience and feels the very flashing of hellfire."[21] If the process stalled at this point, the self was mired in self-loathing—the prototype for our stock notion of the Puritan as a joyless prude, or what we would call a neurotic. But if the process goes forward, a healthy ego begins to take form that incorporates and overcomes guilt. Such spasms of guilt intimate a new ability to see the self, however dimly, as if with the eyes of another. The redeemed soul experiences "a kind of enlargement of the mind, whereby it so extends itself as to take others into a man's self . . . to feel, to desire, and to act as though others were one with ourselves," and thereby it achieves a foretaste (or "prelibation") of salvation.[22]

Here is Jonathan Edwards's famous account of what this transformation meant in his own life:

> I used to be a person uncommonly terrified with thunder; and it used to strike me with terror, when I saw a thunderstorm rising. But now, on the contrary, it rejoiced me. I felt God at the first appearance of a thunderstorm. And used to take the opportunity at such times, to fix myself to view the clouds, and see the lightnings play, and hear the majestic and awful voice of God's thunder . . . And while I viewed, used to spend my time . . . to sing or chant forth my medita-

tions; to speak my thoughts in soliloquies, and speak with a singing voice.[23]

Nobody can teach himself this delight. To some it comes unbidden; to others, despite endless striving, it comes not at all. When it does come, it feels to the melancholy sufferer like a miracle. This is what Puritans meant when they spoke of the grace of God.

ONE REASON these people demanded such an elaborate remapping of the soul was that they found themselves losing their moral bearings in the new world to which they had come. Already in England many had moved out of the planting and harvest rhythms of country life into towns where life was organized according to clock-determined workdays and a weekly sabbath. The goal of subsistence was giving way to the pursuit of profit. What once would have been denounced as usury—lending money at market-rate interest—was becoming a respectable form of investment.

Even in the sanctuary to which they fled, old rules of barter came under pressure from new rules of the marketplace. And so in New England preachers continued to raise such worldly questions as how to set interest rates, when to forgive a loan and when to call it in, or where one's obligation to the poor begins and ends. And though Puritanism has often been described as a businessman's creed, it did not flatter those who achieved worldly success. Never "thinke you have wit enough for your owne businesse," said one minister, or "thinke you deserve all you have." As Edwards remarked a century later, "the hypocrite [always] looks clean and bright in his own eyes."[24]

To puncture the pride of a man puffed up with a sense of his own worthiness, the minister might attack him head on (your "heart is like a dunghill of noysom abominations") or might try to tease him out of his customary channels of thought. When the first-generation minister John Cotton preached that "though Christ cannot be had for money, yet sometimes without expense of money he cannot be had," he was inviting his listeners to puzzle out the paradox that though grace cannot be purchased, it implants a new spirit in the soul that kills old habits of greed and hoarding. (Two centuries later Emerson, whose father had preached to descendants of Cotton's congregation, played similar games with words like "own" and "property": "Miller owns this field, Locke that, and Manning the woodland beyond. But none of them owns the landscape. There is a *property* in the horizon which no man has but he whose eye can integrate all the parts, that is, the poet.") Every conscientious minister knew that in order truly to serve his congregation he had to challenge and chastise them. And so preachers of unusual force and courage inevitably came into conflict with those who paid them to preach—as Edwards did in Northampton, where he was removed from his pulpit by the town worthies when, as Van Wyck Brooks once put it, they "could no longer see the anger of God eye-to-eye with him."[25]

Sermons were not the only weapons against pride. Sacraments, too, were part of the arsenal. In the many conflicts within and between churches over who qualified for baptism and communion, one can see the same struggle to keep pride in check. The privilege of baptism was never understood to confer a guarantee of salvation. As John Davenport, founder of the strict New Haven church, expressed it, grace "is not capable of being propagated . . . in a lineal succession by natural generation." The vocabulary may have been arcane, but the point was plain enough: No one inherits grace. The only thing passed on from generation to generation is sin. Being received into the baptismal covenant is an expression of hope for your soul under the stewardship of the church; but it is never a guarantee that God will find you "comely" to his sight. In fact, the one sure sign of damnation was feeling certain you were saved. In a phrase that nicely prefigured the enduring American hostility toward the idea of inherited privilege, John Cotton wrote: "Do not think that you shall be saved because you are the children of Christian parents."[26]

The ministers I have been describing—I suppose we

might call them America's first public intellectuals—were in the business of training people to become connoisseurs of their own feelings. Yet if we rest with this notion of what they did, we will not have understood much about them—because in the end they distrusted the very feelings they talked so much about. A person might be seized with visions of the bleeding or beckoning Christ, might feel greatly afraid, confused, or enraged; yet in the end, the intensity of one's feelings said nothing about one's spiritual condition. All the elaborate disputations about how, and when, and under what circumstances light or warmth or dizziness or fear might strike the soul were finally beside the point. Whether a feeling comes from God or from a bad meal, the only thing that matters is how it transforms one's relations with other beings—not its internal effects within the self.

HERE WE come to the heart of early American religious culture—and to the roots of a tradition that begins with Cotton and Edwards, runs through Emerson and William James to John Dewey, and, in our own time, finds expression in the work of Richard Rorty and others. This tradition is generally called pragmatism, though I sometimes think it might as well be called Protestantism in the stringent Puritan sense of the word.

Pragmatists do not linger over questions of where

"truth" comes from. Scripture, to be sure, is cited everywhere in Puritan sermons; but it tends to serve the purpose of confirming truth drawn from experience rather than supplying truth *a priori*. Even the Bible-drenched preachers of early New England did not rest their claims on the authority of scripture or on the teachings of famous exegetes; they expected, indeed demanded, that those who listened to them would "go home and consider whether the things that have been taught were true or no"[27]—that they would bring to the Bible not an insolent skepticism but a keen desire to put its teachings to the test of their own lives. In this sense one may speak of the Puritans as proto-pragmatists: they were doubtful that "the worth of a thing can be decided by its origin"[28] and preferred to test any claim to truth by evaluating the *effect* of believing it.

Again James is the best expositor. In *The Varieties of Religious Experience* (1903) (in some respects a self-conscious sequel to Edwards's *A Treatise Concerning Religious Affections*), James makes the essential point: "If the *fruits for life* of the state of conversion are good, we ought to idealize and venerate it, even though it be a piece of natural psychology; if not, we ought to make short work with it, no matter what supernatural being may have infused it." A century and a half earlier, Edwards had made the same point: "Hypocrites may much more easily be brought to talk like saints, than to act like saints," and "holy practice is the chief of all

35

the signs of the sincerity of professors." The only way to know if one has been saved is to see if one lives in a new kind of reciprocal relation with other people.[29]

This conception of what it means to be saved inhabits what is, to my ear at least, one of the most beautiful sentences in all of American literature. It comes from John Winthrop's lay sermon preached aboard the ship that was carrying him to America: "To love and live beloved is the soul's paradise."

What Winthrop has in mind here is not disembodied love. In his letters to his absent wife he aches for her "sweet face . . . and lovely countenance." Using words of great tactility, he does not speak elliptically of her soul, but tenderly of her body. May God keep safe, he tells her (echoing Matthew 10:30), all "the haires of thy head." May God collect "all thy teares in his bottle." In spousal love, as in love of God, the longing for completion involves no calculations of self-interest, but is an unspeakable blessing to the self all the same. Winthrop's words are the American prose equivalent of Adam's poetry in *Paradise Lost* when, even in the face of Eve's mortal sin, he avers his incompleteness without her and vows to stay by her side:

> So forcible within my heart I feel
> The Bond of Nature Draw me to my Own,
> My own in thee, for what thou art is mine;
> Our State cannot be sever'd, we are one,
> One Flesh; to lose thee were to lose myself.[30]

36

What Milton dramatized in *Paradise Lost*, chiefly through Satan's expulsion from paradise but also through Adam's pain at the prospect of life without Eve, is that melancholy is a sinful egotism in which despair and pride reveal themselves as the same thing. This is not merely a significant religious idea; it is the basic motive of all religion. It says to the sufferer, your only deliverance is to discover and submit to something larger and more enduring than yourself. This was the core idea of the first phase of American history— that the radical helplessness disclosed by self-love can only be transcended by loving God, and that love of God is manifest in love of other persons.

I HAVE tried by these remarks to bring us a little closer to people who can seem hopelessly antique and yet strangely current. And while I would not make the effort if I did not think we gain something by trying to see the world as those in the past saw it, something is also thereby lost. In proximity, things disappear that can be better seen from a distance. So there is something to be said for stepping outside the Puritan angle of vision. From outside their perspective we can see more clearly the hypocrisy of their coming to New England seeking religious freedom and then, in short order, banishing or hanging those they deemed heretics. We can see how narrow was their sense of the public when they demanded that Christians "be instru-

ments of publique good in the place where [they]
live"[31]—even as they denied women a public presence
by forbidding them to speak aloud in church. And we
can see, at the same time, how expansive was their
sense of the "place where they lived"—as the Indians
quickly found out.

And so when an irreverent voice breaks through the
official piety it comes as a relief. One appreciates the
military man who, according to an indignant John
Winthrop, announced that God appears to him chiefly
while he smokes tobacco. Or the man who, when an
earnest preacher proclaimed that "the main end of
Planting this Wilderness" was to honor God, called
out, "Sir you are mistaken, . . . our main End was to
catch Fish." And then there is the tenacious Robert
Calef, the Boston merchant who followed the Mathers
(Cotton and his venerable father, Increase) around town
like a paparazzo as they conducted their investigations
into rumors of witchcraft in the 1690s. Here is Calef's
withering account of how closely Cotton Mather exam-
ines a young girl to determine if she is possessed by a
demon: "He . . . rubb'd her stomach (her breast not
covered with the Bed-cloaths) and bid others do so too,
and said it eased her . . ." Watching the scene through
Calef's eyes, we feel closer to him than to the objects of
his satire; he looks upon the clergy rather the way
Monty Python or Mel Brooks might—as if they are

drooling old men using the witch scare as an excuse to fondle girls in public.[32]

In fact, we are more likely to feel at home with just about anyone else in colonial America than with the people I have been talking about. One tires of Samuel Sewall's incessant piety as he writes in his diary that God arranged for him to spill a can of drinking water in bed so he would remember the fragility and brevity of life.[33] There is a peculiar—and in a way, repugnant—mixture of humility and pride in this notion that God (who, you would think, must have been busy with other matters) takes a sufficient interest in any person to arrange the overturning of a watercan as a moral admonition.

Early New England stands at an immense remove from us—and the distance grows steadily larger. Most of us are likely to feel closer to Sewall's Virginia counterpart, William Byrd, who writes in his own (roughly contemporaneous) diary about a different kind of spillage in bed:

> About 3 o'clock I returned to my chambers again and found above a girl who I persuaded to go with me into my chambers but she would not. I ate some cake and cheese and then went to Mr. Bland's where I ate some boiled beef. Then I went to the President's where we were merry till 11 o'clock. Then I stole away. I said a short prayer but notwithstanding committed unclean-

ness in bed. I had good health, bad thoughts, and good humor, thanks be to God almighty.[34]

Or consider that at just about the time Cotton Mather was writing his immense history of God's purposes in founding New England, the *Magnalia Christi Americana,* Byrd's brother-in-law, Robert Beverley, was explaining that Virginia had been founded not by God but by hucksters and swindlers: "They [that is the first promoters] *represented* it as a Scene laid open for the good and gracious Q. *Elizabeth,* to propagate the Gospel in, and extend her Dominions over: As if purposely reserv'd for her Majesty, by a peculiar Direction of Providence . . ."[35]

With Beverley's devastating phrases "they represented it" and "as if purposely reserv'd . . . by . . . Providence," the whole edifice of history as a manifestation of divine will comes crashing down. This man is our forebear and our contemporary more than anyone in early New England. Skeptical about God's immanence, he is less pretentious, and, despite the Puritans' impressive vigilance against pride, finally less self-righteous. He gives us a better preview of melancholy in the modern sense: the suspicion that human beings may be alone in the world, that their claim to be in partnership with the transcendent force of God may be just so much yarnspinning to fill the silence, or, as the cliché goes, so much whistling in the dark. It is not

surprising that some of the most eloquent later expo-
nents of this theme of human aloneness are southern
writers, to one of whom in particular—Walker
Percy—I shall turn for a few moments in the final
chapter.

But if the South was ahead of New England in this
sense, during the eighteenth century New England began to catch up. The Calvinist God receded—first into
various forms of rationalism, then into deism and toward oblivion. In his great works on *The New England
Mind* (1939–1952), Perry Miller called this process
"declension"—a term often misunderstood to mean
that church attendance dropped, or that the number of
religious tracts fell, or that large numbers of people
seceded from religious life altogether. None of these
notions conforms to the facts. Indeed, churches may
even have picked up business as the potent doctrines I
have been talking about gradually lost their force.
(This is the theme of Hawthorne's great story "The
Minister's Black Veil," about a minister who has the
bad taste to reintroduce the idea of sin into what has
become a popular Sunday social hour.)

But however we view the declension question, it is
clear that by 1800, for many who still called themselves Christians, the ideas of original sin and Christ's
compensatory sacrifice had been so weakened that the
whole symbolic system had indeed become quaint. As
the leading Boston Unitarian wrote early in the nine-

teenth century, Calvinism had become a "metaphysical subtility which the mass of people cannot comprehend."[36]

What Puritanism left in its wake will be my subject in the next chapter. For now, let me end with one thought about the odds it faced against surviving in anything like its pure form. Puritanism was an immensely demanding faith. A compressed statement of its essence was given by John Cotton in a nautical metaphor: "The safety of Mariners and Passengers, lives and estates, lyeth not on Ropes or Cables, Anchors, or Ships, Guns or Weapons, but in the name and hand of the Lord; he swadleth and ruleth the Sea."[37]

This is a hard truth to accept at any time or place; and it was especially unwelcome on the cusp of the Enlightenment, when man was just discovering his powers over nature, and, he thought, over himself. Puritanism was not opposed to Enlightenment. (It is good to remember that while Cotton Mather was a believer in witches, he was also an advocate of smallpox inoculation.) But, at its heart, Puritanism had no use for what today we would call human agency. It insisted that human beings could do nothing without God; yet it also insisted that they accept responsibility for themselves. It said that you cannot choose the body into which you are born, or the mind with which you confront the world, or what will happen to you in this life, or to your soul in the next—and yet you are entirely responsible for your fate. Since no one's fate can be separated from the fate of all others, responsibility is never limited to the self. Extending oneself to God through others marks the advent of hope; and while salvation can never be earned, engagement with others is a sign that it may be granted.

This deeply paradoxical faith is still alive in one form or another in America—as it is for the true believers whom I met at AA. But by 1800 it had been permanently displaced from the center of the culture. In the 1830s Emerson declared that "the Puritans in England and America found in the Christ . . . and in the dogmas inherited from Rome, scope for their austere piety and their longings for civil freedom. But their creed is passing away, and none arises in its room."[38] Emerson was right that Puritanism was passing away. But, as we shall see in the next chapter, he was wrong that nothing was arising in its room.

CHAPTER

2

NATION

I ENDED the last chapter with Emerson's report that the old-time religion was dead or dying and that no new faith was coming into view to succeed it. Some would say this report tells more about Emerson's state of mind than about the state of American religion— and they would have a point. Churches were hardly tumbling down (roughly fifty thousand houses of worship were erected between the Revolution and the Civil War), and collection plates circulated more widely than ever (in this period the number of Christian congregations grew three times faster than the population). Yet, amid the din, Emerson "was fain to wrap" himself in his cloak in search of "a solitude that hears not," and to ask a plaintive question: "Where now sounds the persuasion, that by its very melody

47

imparadises my heart, and so affirms its own origin in heaven?"[1]

How many Americans outside the circle of intellectuals shared this yearning for a new "melody" is one of those secrets history will not easily yield up. Contemporary authorities did not agree. While Emerson was convinced that "no man can go with his thoughts about him into one of our churches without feeling that what hold the public worship had on men is gone, or going," others, especially those with personal knowledge of the Old World, were not so sure. For Tocqueville the intense "religious atmosphere of the country was the first thing that struck me on my arrival"—though he seems to have had in mind something more like longing than serenity, and he did "not know if all Americans have faith in their religion—for who can read the secrets of the heart?" When the German theologian Philip Schaff answered a call in 1843 from a seminary in Mercersburg, Pennsylvania, he found that "Christianity . . . [had] even greater power over the mind" in America than in Europe, where it was still "enjoined by civil laws and upheld by police regulations." Frances Trollope, one of a stream of English visitors who crossed the sea as if on a zoological expedition, split the difference along gender lines between those who thought religion was failing and those who thought it alive and well: "I never saw, or read, of any country," she wrote in 1832, "where religion had so strong a hold upon the women, or a slighter hold upon the men."[2]

The point on which everyone did agree was that government was getting out of the business of regulating how citizens could worship. Civil statutes prohibiting blasphemy were falling into disuse, congregations seeking legal incorporation were less likely to be required to conform to any particular creed, and prescribed oaths of office for public officials were evolving toward their modern form, in which such phrases as "almighty God" are embellishments or grace notes.[3] After a last surge in the 1830s, the once-powerful Sabbatarian movement, dedicated to preventing government from compelling its employees "to violate the Lord's day" by moving the mail on Sundays, was reduced from a serious political challenge to a nuisance. (By the 1850s, as the new technology of telegraphy made Sunday mail trains more or less expendable, the sabbath could be honored without much curtailing the transaction of business). In other words, church and state were working out the "amicable separation" that we take for granted today.[4]

With the lifting of civil authority, a burst of spiritual frenzy was released and the United States became what Schaff called "the classic land of sects." If today we live in a celebrity-of-the-week culture, antebellum America was a place where every week seemed to mark the appearance of a fresh prophet determined (to use

Melville's phrase) to "gospelize the world anew." Mormons claimed that an angel named Moroni had brought them golden tablets inscribed by God. Millerites (named for their leader, William Miller) expected the world to end in 1843. A sect under John Humphrey Noyes sought perfection through polygamy—to which they adverted in a slightly leering song about their communal farm at Oneida, New York:

> We have built us a dome
> On our beautiful plantation,
> And we all have one home
> And one family relation.

As for religion in other parts of the country, Emerson heard that down south one could find Methodists "jumping about on all fours, imitating the barking of dogs & surrounding a tree in which they pretended they had '*treed* Jesus.'"[5]

Like many intellectuals since, Emerson regarded the American religious scene as a carnival of crackpots. But traditional religion seemed to him no more satisfying than the new prophets with their promises and nostrums. The very idea of divine creation had been thrown into doubt by the geologist Charles Lyell and the naturalist Robert Chambers, whom we think of now as "pre-Darwinians." From Germany came David Friedrich Strauss's bestselling *Life of Jesus,* news of which preceded its translation into English (1846) by

George Eliot—a book that made belief in the incarnation and the resurrection seem merely credulous. This was the intellectual atmosphere in which Emerson told the graduating class of the Harvard Divinity School in 1838 that "men have come to speak of the revelation as somewhat long ago given and done, as if God were dead." Christianity, he thought, was becoming a "Mythus, as the poetic teaching of Greece and of Egypt, before."[6]

What it left in its wake was unquenched spiritual longing. "Our people," Emerson wrote in his journal a few years before Tocqueville noted the Americans' "strange melancholy in the midst of abundance," "are surrounded with a greater external prosperity & general well-being than Indians or Saxons . . . Yet we are sad & they were not . . . Why should it be? Has not Reflection any remedy for her own diseases?" What Emerson knew of the inner lives of Indians and Saxons might be questioned, but he is always worth listening to on the subject of his own culture: "History gave no intimation of any society in which despondency came so readily to heart as we see it & feel it in ours. Young men, young women at thirty & even earlier seem to have lost all spring & vivacity, & if they fail in their first enterprize the rest is rock & shallow."[7]

And so, as religion split into what he called "corpse-cold" rationalism on the one hand and the phantasmagoria of sects on the other, Emerson joined the crowd of

those seeking a new faith. "I look for the new Teacher
. . . I look for the hour when the supreme Beauty
which ravished the souls of those Eastern men . . . shall
speak in the West also." His shaggy disciple Walt
Whitman summed up the age (with uncharacteristic
succinctness) in a sentence—"the priest departs, the
divine literatus comes"—by which, in the first instance, he meant to announce himself. And Whitman
was explicit about the content of the new faith that was
coming: "The United States themselves," he declared,
"are essentially the greatest poem."[8]

Now what could this oracular pronouncement mean?
How could a political entity deliver the saving power
of religion? And what exactly *was* the United States
anyway?

It is easier to say what it was not. It collected no
income taxes and, until the Civil War, administered no
military conscription. Through the first half of the
nineteenth century its capital city was a fetid little
town without sewers or paved streets, puny enough in
proportion to the grandeur of the national dream that
Whitman thought the "future national capital may . . .
migrate a thousand or two miles" to the West, where it
would be "refounded . . . on a different plan, original,
far more superb." Twenty years earlier, traveling from
New England and New York to Ohio, Tennessee, and

Louisiana, Tocqueville had been impressed by the "irritable patriotism" that made Americans impatient if he criticized any feature of American life, except, perhaps, the weather. In every region he found grand plans for public buildings and monuments—not as commemorations of some past grandeur, but as symbols of the future.[9]

By the 1850s this futuristic state still did not exist in a bureaucratic or administrative sense. It remained an unrealized idea—what William James was later to call a "civic or patriotic utopia"—that promised its citizens the "feeling of being in a wider life than that of this world's selfish little interests." Like any religion, it had a martyrology (revolutionary heroes such as Nathan Hale) and a demonology (Benedict Arnold, Aaron Burr). And as it grew from what Tocqueville called "twenty-four small sovereign nations, whose agglomeration constitutes the body of the Union," into one swaggering country, it acquired a whole mythology of figures half-real and half-imagined—Leatherstocking, Davy Crockett, Brother Jonathan, Yankee Doodle—forebears, all, of Uncle Sam.[10]

What we now think of as classic American literature was one means by which this mythology was created and sustained. The process can be followed from the early hagiographers such as Mason Locke Weems (who elevated the "Swamp Fox" Francis Marion into the

American pantheon, and helped secure a place there for George Washington), through patriotic verse by Longfellow and by Emerson himself (as well as by forgotten poets like Epes Sargent and Francis Miles Finch), to its apotheosis in Edward Everett Hale's once-famous story, "The Man Without a Country" (1863), whose antisecessionist theme was the misery of men exiled "from their country for attempting its ruin."[11]

The development of a genuine literary culture was slowed by residual suspicion of storytelling as a frivolous or corrupting activity (Hawthorne touches on this theme in his preface to *The Scarlet Letter*), by lax copyright laws that allowed established British authors to be pirated by American printers, and by a general taste—characteristic of what today we might call postcolonial cultures—for styles, standards, and even heroes and legends imported from the mother country. Commercially successful authors such as the Anglophile fabulist Washington Irving tended, to use Whitman's contemptuous words, to have had their "birth in courts, and [to have] bask'd and grown in castle sunshine."[12]

It was really not until the 1850s that the fledgling nation produced writers with a claim to a standing in world literature. When they arrived, they were as irreverent and uncontainable as the nation itself. One can hear this in Whitman's all-consuming catalogues that are always reaching for images of inception and always refusing to conclude:

> The carpenter dresses his plank, the tongue of his
>   foreplane whistles its wild ascending lisp . . .
> The machinist rolls up his sleeves . . .
> The half-breed straps on his light boots to compete
>   in the race . . .
> The bugle calls in the ball-room, the gentlemen run
>   for their partners . . .[13]

And one hears it in Melville's whirlwind prose, from which associations tumble out in ceaseless demonstration of how the mind makes fresh experience out of the collision between stored memories and new phenomena:

> Nantucket! Take out your map and look at it . . . Look
> at it—a mere hillock, and elbow of sand: all beach,
> without a background. There is more sand there than
> you would use in twenty years as a substitute for blot-
> ting paper. Some gamesome wights will tell you that
> they have to plant weeds there, they don't grow natu-
> rally; that they import Canada thistles; that they have
> to send beyond seas for a spile to stop a leak in an oil
> cask; that pieces of wood in Nantucket are carried
> about like bits of the true cross in Rome; that people
> there plant toadstools before their houses, to get under
> the shade in summer time; that one blade of grass
> makes an oasis, three blades in a day's walk a prairie;

that they wear quicksand shoes, something like Lap-
lander snow-shoes; that they are so shut up, belted
about, every way inclosed, surrounded, and made an
utter island of by the ocean, that to their very chairs
and tables small clams will sometimes be found adher-
ing, as to the backs of sea turtles. But these extrava-
ganzas only show that Nantucket is no Illinois.[14]

With amazing prescience, Tocqueville had predicted
that democratic literary style would "be fantastic, in-
correct, overburdened . . . loose . . . vehement and
bold," and writers like Whitman and Melville more
than bore him out. They also exemplified a fundamental truth Tocqueville had grasped about America—that
the real nation was to be found not in anything external ("nothing strikes a European traveler in the United
States more than the absence of what we would call
government or administration") but in the outrushing
of the mind by which the American self discovered it
had no boundaries and could consume the world and
turn it into a nutrient of the imagination.[15]

I have been calling this exuberant democracy a new
religion, but, as Whitman rightly said, "all the relig-
ions, old and new," were in it. The bards of the new
democracy converted old religious symbols to novel
purposes, as when Melville used what might be called
the language of transubstantiation to describe the inti-
macy he felt for Nathaniel Hawthorne: "I feel that the
Godhead is broken up like the bread at the Supper, and

that we are the pieces." From the Puritans they inherited the idea that God had struck in America the spark that would ignite a world-purifying fire. (As one New Englander had put it in the 1650s, God caused His "dazzling brightnesse . . . to be contracted in the burning-Glasse of these his peoples zeale, from whence it begins to be left upon many parts of the World with such hot reflection of that burning light . . . till it hath burnt up Babilon Root and Branch.") By 1850 the fire had long been out of control. It had consumed huge stretches of Mexico and was driving the Indians (the new Canaanites) into smaller and smaller pockets of resistance. Whitman predicted that before its bicentennial the United States would have annexed Canada and Cuba.[16]

One famous expression (famous not in his time but in ours) of this "manifest destiny" is a passage from Melville's *White-Jacket:*

We Americans are the peculiar, chosen people—the Israel of our time; we bear the ark of the Liberties of the world. Seventy years ago, we escaped from thrall, and besides our first birth-right—embracing one continent of earth—God has given to us, for a future inheritance, the broad domains of the political pagans, that shall yet come and lie down under the shade of our ark, without bloody hands being lifted. God has predestinated, mankind expects, great things from our race; and great things we feel in our souls . . . And let

57

us always remember that with ourselves, almost for
the first time in the history of earth, national selfish-
ness is unbounded philanthropy; for we can not do a
good to America but we give alms to the world.[17]

I first read these words during the waning days of
the Vietnam War, and they have seemed to me ever
since peculiarly vulnerable to the post-Vietnam irony
that we now bring to all pronouncements of high national purpose. It is hard to recapture the ecstatic spirit
in which they were written. Today we think it scandalous to call the vast North American continent our
"birthright" and to speak of those outside the American circle as "pagans." And yet if there are words in this
passage we might wish to disavow, there are others that
Melville uses in ways we might wish to get back. Lis-
ten, for instance, to the word "race," which he uses in a
loose, nineteenth-century sense that implies no biologically determined identity and has nothing to do
with our own confused notions of the colors and fea-
tures by which we classify human beings. Race, for
Melville, is interchangeable with "nation"—a community to which any individual may belong by virtue of
being born within its boundaries or by the voluntary
acts of emigration and naturalization. As for what he
meant by "philanthropy," it was well summed up by
his contemporary Orestes Brownson, who defined "the
American system" as "the abolition of all artificial dis-

tinctions founded on birth or any other accident," thus leaving "every man to stand on his own two feet, for precisely what God and nature have made him."[18]

Like the zeal to spread it around the globe, this universalist ideal was an inheritance from the old religion—specifically from the doctrine that God, being "no respecter of persons" (Acts 10:34), shows no preference for the lord of the manor over the beggar scratching at his door. Under the old symbolic structure it had been through this unbribable God that ordinary people could feel connected to something larger than themselves. Now a new symbolic system was coming into view that promised something of the same transcendence: "If ever I feel the soul within me elevate and expand to those dimensions not entirely unworthy of its Almighty Architect, it is when I contemplate the cause of my country, deserted by all the world beside, and I standing up boldly alone and hurling defiance at her victorious oppressors."[19] These Promethean words were uttered shortly after Emerson's address at the Harvard Divinity School by a young politician named Abraham Lincoln.

I shall return to Lincoln, but first let me offer one more juxtaposition that may help illustrate the spiritual transmission I am talking about—what Schaff called the "transferring to the civil sphere [of] the idea of the universal priesthood of Christians." Here, from an eighteenth-century Baptist minister, is a passage published in 1750: "That God yet liveth, that passed by the mighty and noble, and chose an *Elisha* from the Plow, and *Amos* from the Herd, and set them to reprove kings." And here, from Melville, is a considerably more famous passage written exactly one hundred years later: "Thou shalt see it shining in the arm that wields a pick or drives a spike; that democratic dignity which, on all hands, radiates without end from God Himself! . . . [who] ever cullest [His] selectest champions from the kingly commons." What had happened in the intervening century was that the God of Augustine and Calvin had become Melville's "great God absolute! the centre and circumference of all democracy!" The spiritual succession for which Emerson had been waiting was under way.[20]

It had, in fact, been prophesied by Tocqueville when he observed that "in democratic communities, the imagination is compressed when men consider themselves; it expands indefinitely when they think of the state." This giddy American was a creature fundamentally different from the peasant or wage laborer of Europe, for whom government was a fearsome parent and who was condemned by history to resent those who stood above him by accident of birth or by some potentate's decree. To the American, by contrast, "government means right," and so he "never obeys another man, but justice, or the law." Except in the plantation South, and in the Hudson valley, where Dutch patroon culture lingered for a while past the Revolution—the feudal stage of social development, with its bitter legacy of class resentment, was a storybook legend rather than a feature of lived experience. In Europe the ordinary man "submits . . . to the caprice of a clerk, but as soon as force is withdrawn . . . [he] vaunt[s] his triumph over the law as over a conquered foe." But in America master and servant "perceive no deep-seated difference between them," and regard their relationship as contractual rather than perpetual. Here was the ground of hope—the idea that Americans were not fixed in their circumstances of birth, but were free to become whatever they could imagine. Knowing that with a small turn of fortune's wheel they may exchange places, the master sees his former self in the servant, and the servant sees his future in the master.[21]

THE aspirations of this new kind of citizen were moderated by what Thomas Jefferson had called "temperate liberty": a capacity for self-government in which the rational understanding acts as a check on the unruly will. And the inner psychological structure of this temperate republican matched the outer system of checks and balances built into the republic itself. For Jefferson temperate liberty was the key to both personal happiness and civil society. It was a "conception of freedom," as Philip Schaff realized, specifically different from the purely negative notion which prevails amongst the radicals and revolutionists of Europe. With the American, freedom is anything but a mere absence of restraint . . . it is a rational, moral, self-determination, hand in hand with law, order, and authority. True national freedom, in the American view, rests upon a moral groundwork, upon the virtue of self-possession and self-control in individual citizens.[22]

With classical ideals of duty and moderation in mind, Jefferson thought that this precious kind of liberty could be cultivated by the affection and discipline of family life, by education focused on the balance and beauty of music, mathematics, and nature, and by religious instruction. But he did not think everyone could acquire it. He was queasy about admitting strangers to his New Jerusalem because he feared they would "bring with them the principles of the [monarchical] governments they leave, imbibed in early youth," and would "infuse into [America] their spirit" of subjection and "licentiousness."[23] And he wondered aloud if the capacity for temperate liberty might somehow be transmitted in the blood.

In his nativism, Jefferson was not unusual. When his fellow Virginian James Madison declared with relief that "kindred blood . . . flows in the veins of American citizens," or when the New Yorker John Jay gave thanks that "Providence has been pleased to give this one connected country, to one united people, a people descended from the same ancestors," it is hard to say just where the metaphor stopped and where a genetic idea of national identity began.[24] In other words, despite its universalist rhetoric of natural rights, the United States was no exception—not only in the South—to what in our own time Hannah Arendt has called "race-thinking." Arendt uses the term *race* not in Melville's nineteenth-century sense but with the horrors of twentieth-century racism in mind: "Race-thinking has been the ever-present shadow accompanying the development of . . . nations."[25] At least in incipient form, this shadow was present at the creation of the republic; and race-thinking not only remained a steady motive and motif in America's imperial expansion but became more strident as political and moral pressure grew against slavery, the domestic institution that most plainly and brutally expressed it.

So the grand claims of our democracy—whether made by the founders or by admiring visitors—were not merely undercut by race-thinking. They were taunted by it. When Jefferson wrote in the 1780s, "I never yet saw a native American begging in the streets or highways," the key word was "native." And yet he knew that by using that word he was begging the crucial questions: How could the sanctity of the self be limited, without being destroyed, to those of "kindred blood"? When, exactly, does an American become an American?[26]

For the immigrant, the answer was in due time, maybe. For the slave, the answer was *never.*

THESE answers were as scandalous as they were accurate, and it is hard to overstate the scale of the scandal, which Schaff called "the restriction and counterpart" to "the American system of general political freedom and equality." Slavery violated the basic premise of democratic individualism as Jefferson himself had announced it: the principle that rights are universal and inalienable. In one of his most remarkable passages, Tocqueville makes the point that the American idea loses all coherence if it admits exceptions:

> I keep asking myself how, in our day, this conception [of rights] may be taught to mankind and made, so as to say, palpable to their senses; and I find one way only, namely, to give them *all* the peaceful use of certain rights. One can see how this works among children . . . [as] when a baby first begins to move among things outside himself, instinct leads him to make use of anything his hands can grasp; he has no idea of other people's property, not even that it exists; but as he is instructed in the value of things and discovers that he too may be despoiled, he becomes more

circumspect, and in the end is led to respect for others that which he wishes to be respected for himself.

Tocqueville then proceeds by analogy from the nursery to the world of adult strife:

> As for a child with his toys, so is it later for a man with all his belongings. Why is it that in America, the land par excellence of democracy, no one makes that outcry against property in general that often echoes through Europe? Is there any need to explain? It is because there are no proletarians in America. Everyone, having some possession to defend, recognizes the right to property in principle.[27]

Here is the seed of what is sometimes called the "consensus" school of American historiography—the idea that in a nation where everyone has possessions to defend, any movement hostile to property rights will have only enemies, no friends.

On this unexamined premise, conservatives have delighted in Tocqueville's vision of a bourgeois paradise, and have claimed him as one of their own. It is true that he was impressed by the degree to which civil society in America seemed to depend on the vitality of local associations and to thrive in the absence of a centralized state apparatus. But liberals, I think, should claim him as well—because he insisted that civil society depends at least as much on a fair distribution of wealth. In this sense, he hinted at a larger conception of rights than what we now sometimes call "procedural" or "negative" rights, and he realized that the one thing fatal to democracy is a class of people without hope.

Here, moreover, is the clue to why Tocqueville sent himself to the New World in the first place. He (and his traveling companion, Gustave de Beaumont) came with the specific intent of studying American penal institutions, but the book that emerged from their travels was driven by a larger motive. It was born out of Tocqueville's family's experience during the revolutionary years in France. There is a suggestive hint to this effect in a report from an English friend who, while visiting Tocqueville in 1850 at his ancestral home in Normandy, noticed that Alexis's father, who had been imprisoned during the Terror, retired to sleep every afternoon between three and four o'clock so he would not be tormented by the waking memory of how the guards came faithfully at that hour to his cell to select a prisoner for the day's quota at the guillotine. For the old man's son, America was the place where such horrors could not happen. It was the country where no citizen need fear the approaching sound of the hobnail boot.[28]

Tocqueville was an emigrant to this New World only in his imagination (his visit lasted nine months); but surely these passages have a special force for any

American reader who still feels close to the experience of a parent or grandparent who fled to this country from some Old World hell. I found myself thinking this not long ago in a New York taxicab festooned with stars-and-stripes decals, when the immigrant driver explained to me that he blessed his adopted country as a sanctuary from fear. In America, he said, one need not be afraid of the police. This taxi driver was, of course, white.

I say "of course," because a great many black people—newcomers and longtime citizens—would demur at his claim, and they would be right to do so. One simply cannot read Tocqueville on the Old World man who "oscillates between servility and license" without being reminded that fear and rage of the sort he thought was becoming extinct in America remain today a constituent part of the black experience. Reading his description of the sullen Old World man who bows to the government clerk with nothing of a citizen's consent is bound, I think, to bring to mind the iconic image of a smoldering young black man in handcuffs. It reminds us of the shame of American history—that one hundred thirty-five years after emancipation, Tocqueville's Old World continues to be part of our New World, and that its color is still predominantly black.

The indispensable insight of *Democracy in America* is that democracy thrives only if it sees to the universal distribution of hope. In the America Tocqueville visited, hope stopped at the color line. For too many Americans, it still does.[29]

AMONG OUR classic writers, it was Melville who felt this truth most deeply. He brings it into view when he describes Ishmael, on his journey to cure himself of the "hypos," seeing for the first time the ship on which he will pursue his destiny. Here is what Ishmael says: "She was a thing of trophies . . . a cannibal of a craft, tricking herself forth in the chased bones of her enemies." Her tiller, he notices, is carved with a whale's jaw, and her bulwarks are studded with the teeth of the great whales she has chased, killed, and boiled into the stuff she is bringing to market for making perfume and for filling a thousand lamps with oil. Like America itself, the Pequod is a world-conquering ship. And Ishmael's awe before her is animated, as genuine awe must always be, by terror as well as by love: "A noble craft," he says of her, "but somehow a most melancholy! All noble things are touched with that."[30]

Allegorized in the Pequod was the dirty secret of the new national religion—the fact that the ebullient democracy was also a killing machine. It killed the hope for freedom in the black people whom it had imported to do its work ("the native American liberally provides the brains," as Melville describes the *Pequod's* officers and crew, while "the rest of the world as generously suppl[ies] the muscles").[31] With all its promise, the

New World had its novel savageries and forms of despair.

The central drama of American history has been the struggle to force these savageries into view. Jefferson did not see them when he sat in his Monticello study writing that "those that labor in the earth are the chosen people of God" (by which he meant white yeoman farmers) without, apparently, ever looking out the window at his field slaves. Most Americans still did not see them seventy years later when Frederick Douglass, the first black American to achieve international standing as an advocate for the enslaved, spoke in Rochester on the 5th of July, 1852, and said, "Your celebration is a sham . . . your denunciation of tyrants [is] brass fronted impudence . . . your prayers and hymns, your sermons and thanksgivings, with all your religious parade and solemnity, are, to Him, mere bombast, fraud, deception, impiety, and hypocrisy."[32]

The day of reckoning with this truth was repeatedly postponed. It was postponed when Jefferson's self-contradictory grievance clause over the perpetuation of the slave trade was excised from the Declaration. It was put off again when slavery was written into the Constitution. The process of deferral continued with the Missouri Compromise of 1820 and the arduously negotiated Compromise of 1850, which tried to restore the balance of power between slave states and free states that had been periodically disturbed by territorial expansion. It was deferred and delayed, deflected and evaded—until November 1860, when a man was elected president on the platform of stopping the spread of slavery and putting it, as he said, "in the path of ultimate extinction."[33]

IN THE life of Abraham Lincoln the themes I have been discussing are recapitulated and brought to completion. He himself seems to have been afflicted with a chronic melancholy that, in the words of one biographer, subjected him to "black despondency and boisterous humor following one another like cloud and sunshine in a day of doubtful storm." According to his friend Billy Herndon, "melancholy dripped from him as he walked."[34] He felt, with Emerson, that he had been born too late. After an unremarkable career as a state legislator and congressman, he retreated from public life (in 1848) and seemed destined to spend the remainder of his days as a litigator of merely local repute. But when, in 1854, the Kansas-Nebraska Act opened the territories to slavery, and repealed, as he thought, the Missouri Compromise, he was "thunderstruck and stunned." He was "aroused as [he] had never been aroused before," and undertook to return to active politics on the principle first of containing slavery, then of eradicating it.[35]

Abraham Lincoln was a reluctant abolitionist. In fact, strictly speaking, he was never an abolitionist at all. Even when he signed the Emancipation Proclamation at the height of the Civil War in 1863, slavery remained legal where it had hitherto existed in slave states not in rebellion against the Union (Delaware, Missouri, Kentucky, and Maryland). He fended off demands before and during the war that he act against slavery where it existed; and he insisted, again and again, that the Constitution empowered him only to arrest its spread. Yet he never wavered in his hatred of it. "I hate it," he said, "because of the monstrous injustice of slavery itself. I hate it because it deprives our republican example of its just influence in the world—enables the enemies of free institutions, with plausibility, to taunt us as hypocrites." That taunting had been going on at least since Samuel Johnson (who had a keen nose for hypocrisy) demanded to know, during the revolutionary war, "How is it that the loudest cries for liberty come from the drivers of Negroes?"[36]

Today it is possible, and even fashionable, to discount the manifest intensity of Lincoln's hatred of slavery. It is true that he acknowledged, and possibly to some extent shared, what he called "the natural disgust in the minds of nearly all white people, to the idea of an indiscriminate amalgamation of the races," yet Frederick Douglass once remarked on Lincoln's "entire freedom from popular prejudice against the colored race."[37] Still, it was not just Lincoln's personal freedom from prejudice that distinguished him. He had an astounding ability to lead his listeners inward by words, away from pseudo-scientific theories about black inferiority, toward their core sense of outrage at the arrogance of power. He had an instinctive feeling for the plight of the slave looking northward, as Douglass had described it: "At every gate through which we had to pass, we saw a watchman; at every ferry a guard; on every bridge, a sentinel; and in every wood, a patrol or slave-hunter. We were hemmed in on every side."[38]

Two years after Douglass wrote those words, Lincoln echoed them, perhaps unwittingly, when he spoke about the *Dred Scott* decision in the proverbial capital of the American heartland, Peoria, Illinois:

All the powers of the earth seem rapidly combining against [the Negro]. Mammon is after him; ambition follows, and philosophy follows, and the Theology of the day is fast joining the cry. They have him in his prison house; they have searched his person, and left no prying instrument with him. One after another they have closed the heavy iron doors upon him, and now they have him, as it were, bolted in with a lock of a hundred keys, which can never be unlocked without the concurrence of every key; the keys in the hands of a hundred different men, and they scattered to a hundred different and distant places; and they stand musing as to what invention, in all the dominions of mind and matter, can be produced to make the impossibility of his escape more complete than it is.[39]

It may be true that Lincoln conceded—possibly in-genuously, probably for tactical reasons—to prevailing racial attitudes. But it is, I think, a truth of more consequence that, in studying what the founding fa-thers had said about race and slavery, he committed what Harold Bloom might call an act of "strong misreading" on behalf of his hatred of slavery. He con-strued the founders as resolute anti-slavery men—not-withstanding the fact that many of them were slaveowners, and relatively insouciant ones at that.[40] Despite Jefferson's having written that black people's inability to blush or blanch was a sign that they lived a primitive emotional life, Lincoln decided that the authentic Thomas Jefferson was the man who wrote that "all men are created equal." The document that meant everything to him ("the apple of gold" within the silver frame of the Constitution," as he called it) was the Declaration of Independence.[41] By the end of his life he saw himself as having been appointed to complete the promise that Jefferson had left un-fulfilled.

Edmund Wilson once argued that Lincoln believed he was born to be a great avenger. I find this argument rather overwrought; but Lincoln did sometimes speak with an almost Calvinistic sense of being in the grip of what his forebears would have called providence. "I claim not to have controlled events," he wrote to the Kentucky journalist Albert Hodges, "but confess plainly that events have controlled me." He spoke as if some irresistible force behind events were propelling him toward a destiny that involved much more than his own life.[42]

And this is why we remember him. We do not remember him for his conventional Whig vision of a prosperous republic linked by railroads and canals. We remember him not for his vision of prosperity but for his passion for justice. Lincoln's model American was a descendant of Ben Franklin and a forebear of the Horatio Alger newsboy, a "prudent, penniless beginner in the world, [who] labors for wages awhile, saves a surplus with which to buy tools or land for himself, then labors on his own account another while, and at length hires another new beginner to help him." What made Lincoln different from previous tellers of the rags-to-riches tale (and it was a very big difference) was his insistence that "I want every man to have [this] chance—and I believe a black man is entitled to it" too.[43] The lesson of Lincoln's life—the life he lived, and the life that endures in our national memory—is that the quest for prosperity is no remedy for melancholy, but that a passion to secure justice by erasing the line that divides those with hope from those without hope can be.

Let me summon another Concord Transcendentalist as a witness to this truth. When Henry David Thoreau heard of John Brown's martyrdom in 1859, he wrote,

74

"These men, in teaching us how to die, have at the same time taught us how to live . . . How many a man who was lately contemplating suicide has now something to live for!"[44] As far as we know, Abraham Lincoln never contemplated suicide (the stories of his despair at the death of his first love, Anne Rutledge, are not reliable), and he was on record as believing that John Brown was a fanatic. And yet he expressed his passion for justice in a way that accords with Thoreau's idea that life is worth living only when it furnishes the mind with something worth dying for. En route to Washington for his first inauguration amid rumors of a plot to kill him, Lincoln stopped at Philadelphia, where, standing in Independence Hall, he said, "I have never had a feeling politically that did not spring from the sentiments embodied in the Declaration of Independence." Then, with eerie foresight, he added that before he would save the Union by giving up those principles, he "would rather be assassinated on this spot."[45]

Among the most remarkable of his writings is a brief meditation, possibly a memo for a speech or a jotting for his own later consideration, composed around 1854. It expresses his proto-modern insight that the very idea of race (notwithstanding its growing prestige in nineteenth-century "science" and the inroads it may have made into his own mind) is incoherent and indefensible. He saw, as we would say today, that it is a "socially constructed" idea. He saw that no one has ever really understood what "race" is, and that, in the end, it is whatever powerful people say it is:

> If A. can prove, however conclusively, that he may, of right enslave B.—why may not B. snatch the same argument, and prove equally, that he may enslave A?—
>
> You say A., is white, and B. is black. It is *color,* then; the lighter, having the right to enslave the darker?
>
> Take care. By this rule, you are to be slave to the first man you meet, with a fairer skin than your own.
>
> You do not mean *color* exactly?—You mean the whites are *intellectually* the superiors of the blacks, and therefore have the right to enslave them? Take care again. By this rule, you are to be slave to the first man you meet, with an intellect superior to your own.
>
> But, say you, it is a question of *interest;* and, if you can make it your *interest,* you have the right to enslave another. Very well. And if he can make it his interest, he has the right to enslave you.

This is Lincoln's completion of Tocqueville's little parable of the child learning that it is in his own interest to respect the property rights of other children. Lincoln knew it was fatally dangerous *to oneself* to deny to others the rights one claims as one's own.[46]

In the last analysis, Lincoln regarded the hope of building one's dignity on another man's degradation not merely as an error but as a sin. (Here, in prospect, is the theme Mark Twain would personify in Huck Finn's Pap—the bitter hope that somewhere there is someone doomed to stoop lower than oneself, someone upon whose back one can rest one's dignity.) Since northerners financed the slave trade and owned the textile mills, it was a sin he refused to impute only to the people of the South. He was not a conventionally religious man (he had once been charged by a political rival with being an infidel). But in Lincoln's imagination we see most clearly the theme I have broached in this chapter—the process by which Christian symbolism, even as it was weakening, was transformed into the symbol of a redeemer nation, and, thereby, into a new symbol of hope.

That process was two hundred years old when Lincoln completed it. In the 1650s the Puritan poet Michael Wigglesworth wrote in his diary, "I feel a need of Christ's blood to wash me from [my] sins"; in the 1850s Lincoln wrote in his speech on the Kansas-Nebraska Act, "Our republican robe is soiled, and trailed in the dust. Let us repurify it. Let us turn and wash it white, in the spirit, if not the blood of the Revolution." Seven years and hundreds of thousands of deaths later, he said in his Second Inaugural Address that slavery was a sin that God had willed to be expiated by blood—"till every drop of blood drawn with the lash, shall be paid by another drawn with the sword."[47] Delivered in the midst of what had become for Lincoln a holy war, the Second Inaugural is the purest instance in American oratory of religious fervor transmuted into a secular crusade. With magnanimity for the enemy but with unrelenting enmity for the enemy's cause, Lincoln saw Americans on both sides of the battle lines as bearers of a tragic inheritance. He cut through the cant about property rights and states' rights and identified slavery as the indisputable cause of a war that had revealed itself as the providential means by which the nation could be bled free of the slave poison.

With all his hedging about racial equality, and all his reticence about what Americans might owe to one another beyond a fair chance in the marketplace, Lincoln exemplified Thoreau's insight that there can be no greater miracle than "for us to look through each other's eyes for an instant." What he apprehended, however fleetingly, through the eyes of the slave, was, in the words of Frederick Douglass, "the thought of only being a creature of the *present* and the *past*," and a longing "to have a *future*—a future with hope in it."[48] Lincoln called this hope the Union—the idea, as Alexander Stephens, Vice President of the Confederacy, put it, that "rose for him to the sublimity of religious mysticism." For Lincoln the Union was both symbol and incarnation of transcendence. It is in that sense that he brought to fruition both the religious idea I discussed in the first chapter and the idea of the nation I have discussed in this one.[49]

It is sometimes remarked that Lincoln was America's version of Mazzini or Bismarck—a man who, by sheer force of will, forged a unitary nation out of a multiplicity of mini-states. The analogy is not far-fetched, but it is misleading, because the forces that have played so large a part in the modern reconfiguration of Europe—ethnic, religious, and linguistic solidarity—were, for Lincoln, not merely subsidiary but inimical to the idea of the Union by which he was possessed. Lincoln's Union was neither conceived as the reclamation of ancestral lands nor faithful to the root meaning of the word "nation," which derives from the Latin *natio,* to be born, and implies a fidelity to parentage that transcends all other loyalties. Lincoln's nation had nothing to do with such genealogical ideas as *Volk* or *patria.* It was, instead, the political incarnation of the idea of universal rights—of a new age when people who cannot "trace their connection . . . by blood" to the birth of the nation nevertheless are as fully American as if "they were blood of the blood, and flesh of the flesh" of the founders.[50]

Immediately after his death Lincoln began to undergo the transformation into martyrdom ("a new era was born," said one eulogist, "and made perpetual through his death")[51] that made him the central figure

in America's historical understanding of itself. He became the key symbol of the idea of universal rights and
the most eloquent witness to the tragedy of its be-
trayal, and thereby established himself at the center of
our national story. The question to which I shall turn
in the final chapter is whether that center still holds.

CHAPTER

3

SELF

HERE, to borrow a phrase from Governor Bradford, "I must stay and make a pause." I have tried not to overindulge in what one of Bradford's contemporaries called "the fond admiration of former times"—that mood of melancholy belatedness that afflicts our literature from the moment the first Puritans landed in Massachusetts Bay, where, before the soil of Old England was off their boots, they were extolling "the cheapnesse . . . great hospitality . . . kind neighbourhood . . . [and] valiant acts" of "*former* times," and fretting that there were "no such now a dayes."[1]

Reading those old laments has a certain therapeutic value, since it turns out that everything we think today has been thought before—especially the dark thought that the world is in unprecedented trouble. If we worry that the presidency has fallen on evil times, it helps to remember that Henry Adams was convinced more than a hundred years ago that "the progress of evolution from President Washington to President Grant, was alone evidence enough to upset Darwin." If we think the civic fabric is coming apart, it helps to find Emerson saying so a long time ago: "Every man [is] for himself . . . the social sentiments are weak; the sentiment of patriotism is weak; veneration is low . . . there is an universal resistance to ties and ligaments once supposed essential to civil society." Emerson ticks off here just about every sign of civil decay we would be likely to find today in a catalogue of lamentations (as compiled, say, by Amitai Etzioni or Robert Putnam), except that people have dropped out of their bowling leagues in favor of bowling alone.[2]

In fact, it is easy, and fun, to gather such jeremiads by the bushel. Today they come from the left, as when Gore Vidal remarks that the "*McGuffey's Readers* of my grandfather's day would now be considered intolerably high-brow"; from the right, as when William Bennett rails against fallen educational standards; and from what Arthur Schlesinger Jr. once called the "vital center," when he warns against the "disuniting" of America. Where the breakpoint falls between the worthy past and the unworthy present often depends on when the Jeremiah himself was young. So the movie-star-turned-director Robert Redford locates the end of public trust in the quiz show scandals of the 1950s, and the novelist Don DeLillo thinks "the last time people went spontaneously out of their houses for . . . wonder [and] amazement" was when Bobby Thomson hit an inside fastball off Ralph Branca into the left field seats at the Polo Grounds on October 3, 1951.[3]

It is true that every jeremiad feeds on nostalgia; but it is also true, as T. Jackson Lears has pointed out, that "visions of the good society can come from recollections and reconstructions of the past, not only from fantasies of the future."[4] So, unrepentant of my taste for the genre, let me offer one last example before I launch into a jeremiad of my own.

I have a special affection for this one, since I am, of course, against the designated-hitter rule as a means to keep over-the-hill baseball players in the game, against using "middle" relievers and "closers" as a way of coddling starters who lack stamina, against Astroturf as a way to turn ground-outs into base hits, against short fences that favor Mark McGwire, against long between-inning breaks to make time for TV commercials, against electronic scoreboards, indeed against just about everything that has happened to baseball since the Second World War—with the possible exception of night games. Having said that, let me offer what one baseball historian calls a "doomsday ditty," about which the only surprising thing is that it was composed in 1886, when the game had barely been invented:

Oh, don't you remember the game of base-ball we saw
  twenty years ago played,
When contests were true, and the sight free to all,
  and home-runs in plenty were made?
When we lay on the grass, and with thrills of delight,
  watched the ball squarely pitched at the bat,
And easily hit, and then mount out of sight along
  with our cheers and our hat?
And then, while the fielders raced after the ball, the
  men on the bases flew round,
And came in together—four batters in all. Ah! That
  was the old game renowned.

Now salaried pitchers, who throw the ball curved at
  padded and masked catchers lame
And gate-money music and seats all reserved is all that
  is left of the game.
Oh, give us the glorious matches of old, when love of
  true sport made them great.
And not the new-fashioned affair always sold for the
  boodle they take at the gate.[5]

Now, if America has always seemed in decline, even
at times that we now recall as innocent and eager, then
the proverbial question arises—What else is new? All
of us have a full shelf of books with titles announcing
The End of this or The Death of that (I have written
such a book myself); just in the several months I have
been at work on this book, Henry Louis Gates Jr. announced in the *New Yorker* "the end of loyalty" and

William Safire lamented in the *New York Times* "the death of outrage."[6] If we have been going to hell since the first landfall at Plymouth, what makes today any different? To ask this question is to skip over more than one hundred years of history from where I stopped at the close of the previous chapter—so let me take a few moments to try to justify this rather extravagant leap.

THE HISTORY of the United States from Lincoln's death to the wave of assassinations in the 1960s can be seen, I think, as a struggle to realize Lincoln's vision of an entrepreneurial society whose citizens are unencumbered by parentage or origin. The struggle to secure this chance for all Americans has been bitter and bloody, and it is far from over. After Lincoln's death the Fourteenth Amendment grandly promised that the power of the federal Union would guarantee the rights of all persons against infringement by the states; but this guarantee was exploited by business corporations (which the courts construed as "juridical persons") while remaining a hollow pledge to millions of actual persons. Women did not get the vote until five amendments later, and their legal rights, as Tocqueville had noticed in the 1830s, were often "lost in the bonds of matrimony."[7] As for blacks, their gains were virtually repealed in the reaction against Reconstruction, and political equality remained mostly a sham until the passage of the Voting Rights Act a hundred years after Lincoln's death. The truncation of Lincoln's vision in his own time and ours is vividly apparent in the fact that there is no more ferocious debate today than over the question of why blacks still lag behind whites by most measures of economic success.

The struggle to realize Lincoln's ideal was waged not only by workers against capital but also by workers against other workers—against immigrants (and, as always, against blacks) who formed the next wave of what Lincoln had called "prudent [and] penniless" beginners. In less than one human life span following the Civil War, the United States absorbed a staggering influx of immigrants whose first means to upward mobility was often organized crime (a good introduction, Daniel Bell once called it, to "the American Way of Life"),[8] and who found that social services, such as they were, were dispensed by a political patronage system that ran on graft. The risk of injury, disease, and early death—hazards inherent in the brutal transformation of America into a great industrial power—went largely unacknowledged, forcing millions to rely on themselves, on family, and on the charity of friends.

To some who watched the immigrants pour in, it seemed that America would have to reorganize itself according to the "multicultural" principle that we hear so much about today. The term was first given currency by Horace Kallen, who wrote in *The Nation* in 1915 that, with the growth of large immigrant communities, the rate of mixed marriage would drop (he was wrong) and the "likelihood of a new 'American' race" would decline. The United States, he predicted, would turn into "a democracy of nationalities" in which "selfhood . . . is ancestrally determined." To other observers, the country was simply sliding into chaos, as it seemed to Henry Adams in 1905 when he "looked out of the club window on the turmoil of Fifth Avenue and felt himself in Rome, under Diocletian, witnessing the anarchy."[9]

As one looks back on these pronouncements, it is not always easy to distinguish the motive of reform from a certain prissy dismay at the foreign-flavored urban mess. There is an American tradition in which reform appears chiefly as a form of self-therapy—a tradition crystallized in Thoreau's mordant remark that "what so saddens the reformer is not his sympathy with his fellows in distress, but . . . his private ail," and running from Hawthorne's satire of Brook Farm in *The Blithedale Romance* (1852), through Henry James's portrayal of feminists as neurotics in *The Bostonians* (1886), to Van Wyck Brooks's quip (made in 1915) that Andrew Carnegie spent "three quarters of his life in providing steel for battleships and the last quarter of it in trying to abolish war."[10]

All these writers have a point. But one could put the matter differently and say, with Pericles, that "the last pleasure, when one is worn out with age, is not . . . making money, but having the respect of one's fellow men."[11] For many people—rich, middling, and poor—self-fulfillment paradoxically depends on exercise of what Edith Wharton, writing with gentle mockery in 1905, called the "other-regarding sentiments." John Jay Chapman, writing around the same time, made the same point, but with growling generosity: "The veneration for hospitals is not accorded to them because they cure the sick, but because they stand for love, and responsibility."[12] In other words, the good society cannot exist without institutions built on the principle of service rather than profit. It must provide for its losers, not only for their sake, but, if I may put it anachronistically, for the sake of the souls of the winners.

This communitarian countertheme to American individualism had been, I believe, implicit in Lincoln's vision of a sacred republic. It was revived by quasi-religious orders such as the Salvation Army and the Red Cross, which mimicked the military discipline of the Civil War, as well as in the broader ameliorative program that came to be known as the Social Gospel. Even as Americans lived more and more by the logic of the marketplace, revulsion was building at the life of untempered greed—a disgust that was as evident in the writings of such stringent Protestants as Carnegie and John D. Rockefeller, who thought of themselves, however improbably, as crusaders against cupidity, as it was in the writings of reformers such as Jane Addams, Lincoln Steffens, or Henry George.[13]

Here was the seed of the modern liberal state. When exactly that seed was planted is a matter of continuing debate; some historians detect it in the anti-trust laws of the 1890s; others find it germinating earlier, in federal programs for supporting Civil War veterans and widows.[14] Wherever we first discern it, it expressed not only tactical concessions by the rich but also an inner compulsion for justice—and even, to use Chapman's religiously tinged word, for mercy. "At the core of democracy," Whitman said, "is the religious element."[15] What Christianity and democracy share is the idea that to live in a purely instrumental relation with other human beings, to exploit and then discard them, is to give in entirely to the predatory instinct and to leave unmet the need for fellowship and reciprocity. For too many people, this need seems to be satisfied by low forms of tribalism or cliquishness; but it is both sentimental and dogmatic to imagine that it belongs in its higher forms only to the poor and never to the rich.

I see no reason to doubt—and I do not think history supports such doubt—that human beings of all classes and all cultures have this need for contact with what William James called the "Ideal Power" through which that "feeling of being in a wider life than that of this world's little interests" may be reached: "In Christian saintliness this power is always personified as God; but abstract moral ideals, civic or patriotic utopias, or inner visions of holiness or right may also be felt as the true Lords and enlargers of our life."[16] The United States has never been a "civic . . . utopia." Far from it. But it has been the scene of a struggle for justice within the terms adumbrated by Jefferson and carried forward, though left incomplete, by Lincoln. Before the New Deal, the institutions and symbols that arose out of and sustained this faith in a better future were chiefly private (churches, hospitals, settlement houses, orphanages); but Lincoln—perhaps more through his death than through his life—contributed immeasurably to the sacralization of the state as the source of justice, mercy, and hope.

The question we face today is how, or whether, this "feeling of being in a wider life" is still available. Can the nation-state still provide it? If not, what can?

UNTIL our own time, the history I have just raced through—as exfoliated in Progressivism, the New Deal, and the Great Society—was understood within a paradigm of moral progress. Depending on when or by whom it was written, it was said to have moved from, say, Dred Scott to the Emancipation Proclamation to *Brown v. Board of Education,* or from the Triangle Shirtwaist Company factory fire to the adoption of workplace regulation. It was, moreover, a story flexible enough to accommodate setbacks such as the *Plessy v. Ferguson* decision confirming second-class citizenship for blacks, as if these were standard deviations from the progressive norm. And whatever particular form it took, it was written with confidence (call it Hegelian, or Edwardsean) that an inner rationality was driving our history toward national self-realization in the form of universal human rights.

Today this story is in trouble in a way it has never been before. It still has some life in it—as in the emerging field of gay history, in which the key signposts lead from colonial sodomy laws through the Stonewall "riot" to the pending legalization of gay marriage; or in the rising arc of women's history from enfranchisement, through public acceptance of birth control, into the continuing struggle for abortion rights. New stories are also beginning to be told according to the same sequence of enslavement followed by deliverance: for instance, the story of how disabled people are coming out of their long confinement between shame and pity to within hailing distance of dignity, as heralded by the most significant piece of social legislation passed during the Bush administration, the Americans with Disabilities Act of 1990.[17]

But for reasons to which I now want to turn, discrete stories of particular groups within American society tend no longer to be regarded as tributaries that come together in a collective national history of expanding rights. As the cultural critic Bill Readings wrote, we "no longer tell a story of liberation as the passage from the margins to the center."[18] It is impossible to date the death of this story with any precision; but if we look somewhere around the moment when the reformist dream that Lyndon Johnson called the Great Society became a casualty of the Vietnam war, we will not, I think, be too far off the mark.[19]

It was at the height of that tragic war, in 1967, that Robert Bellah published a famous (and, in some quarters, notorious) essay in which he argued that the mysterious coherence and enormous power of the United States had been secured and expressed through what he called a "civil religion," whose central figure he properly identified as Abraham Lincoln. For Bellah this "set of beliefs, symbols, and rituals" (individual rights, the Supreme Court, the Capitol dome, the mansion in which the president lives at the people's pleasure, the whole panoply of public ceremonies—parades, inaugurations, conventions) represented an "articulation between the profoundest commitments of the Western religious and philosophical tradition and the common beliefs of ordinary Americans."[20]

I have tried in these chapters to reveal something of the complexity of that articulation, to give some sense of its elaboration through time, and to suggest how it arose from the unquenchable human need to feel connected to something larger than the insular self. Now I want to turn to the question of whether Bellah was describing a symbolic system that remains vital and continues to evolve at the end of the twentieth century, or whether he was writing its obituary.

LET US approach this question through a text. I have in mind a beautiful passage in Whitman's memoir *Specimen Days,* in which he recalls stopping in front of the White House on a mild February evening in 1863 when he was working as a nurse in a Washington hospital. In it he renders the White House as a luminous symbol of hope:

> The white portico—the palace-like, tall, round columns, spotless as snow—the walls also—the tender and soft moonlight, flooding the pale marble, and making peculiar faint languishing shades, not shadows—everywhere a soft transparent hazy, thin, blue moon-lace, hanging in the air—the brilliant and extra-plentiful clusters of gas, on and around the facade, column, portico, &c.—everything so white, so marbly pure and dazzling yet soft—the White House of future poems, and of dreams and dramas, there in the soft and copious moon.

If Whitman's "dreams and dramas" have lately turned to farce, it is not because the rascality of our leaders is any greater than it once was. Nor has some hitherto unwavering civic tact suddenly given way. Two hundred years ago, Jefferson was accused (apparently accurately, according to genetic tests on his descendants) of producing bastard children with his slave mistress; Andrew Jackson's wife was publicly reviled as a slut; Franklin Roosevelt's sons were denounced during the Second World War for getting army desk assignments far from the risks of combat. The collapse of public trust in the integrity of government (one point on which pollsters of both parties agree) has deeper sources than the actual misbehavior of politicians.[21]

When was it first discernible? Perhaps one could hear it coming in the eerie whine of Jimi Hendrix's electric-guitar version of "The Star Spangled Banner" at Woodstock in 1969, though that performance still had the sound of an erstwhile believer whose hope had been betrayed. Or perhaps, like the burning out of a supernova, the civil religion reached a death-climax in the hyperpatriotism of the Reagan years, when Mr. Reagan liked to decorate the Puritans' favorite phrase from scripture, "city on a hill," with the gratuitous word "shining"—a participle that St. Matthew and John Winthrop had been content to do without.

Something died, or at least fell dormant, between the later 1960s, when the reform impulse subsided into solipsism, and the 1980s—two phases of our history that may seem far apart in political tone and personal style, but that finally cooperated in installing instant gratification as the hallmark of the good life, and in repudiating the interventionist state as a source of hope. What was lost in the unholy alliance between an insouciant New Left and an insufferably smug New Right was any conception of a common destiny worth tears, sacrifice, and maybe even death. Patriotism, some say, persists in the "heartland" (wherever that mythic region may now be), but among people of "advanced" views it has lost respectability as surely as did traditional religion in Emerson's day. Once one gets past the gestural difference between flag waving and nose thumbing, it is hard to find, on the right or the left, anything resembling genuine engagement with the life of the polity.

Such engagement is rare because it requires a collective vision of a better future, which has become even rarer. What passes today for such a vision from intellectuals on the right is the specter of a *Clockwork Orange* megalopolis interrupted here and there by gated communities of the rich, while from the left—chastened by the collapse of Marxism abroad and the retrenchment of the welfare state at home—we get mainly silence, or a lot of theoretical talk about the hegemony of bourgeois culture. In science fiction, where one would expect the futuristic imagination to be on full display, the community-minded robots of Isaac Asimov have been replaced by the cyberpunks of William Gibson. Even the Disney "imagineers" cannot seem to figure out what to do with that part of the park called Tomorrowland; built in the 1950s as a model technological utopia, it has become a hokey replica of a stage set for the Jetsons, and no one seems able to conceive a new edition.[22]

Sixty years ago, the Boys Athletic League of New York conducted a survey of 50,000 children between the ages of six and sixteen on the question, "Who do you think is the most loved man in the world?" In that poll, God finished second to Franklin D. Roosevelt.[23] Last year, I heard a pediatrician remark that over his thirty years of practice the children he treats have become less and less responsive to his standard question, "What do you want to be when you grow up?" In the past he got lots of answers following the formula "I want to be like _____," with the name of a sports hero, or a scientist, or even a politician filling in the blank. Now he gets a shrug, or an "I dunno," or, sometimes, the name of a TV cartoon character. Nothing, it seems to me, is more alarming than the impoverishment of our children's capacity to imagine the future.

Graham Greene once defined melancholy as the "logical belief in a hopeless future." Lionel Trilling once called it "the diminution of belief in human possibility."[24] For us, I think, these definitions hit close to home—because life seems, as in the favorite prefix of our post-industrial, post-modern, post-national, post-theistic age, just plain *post-*.

Here is an exemplary stretch of dialogue from a

prophet of our "post-" condition. It is an exchange from Walker Percy's novel *Love in the Ruins,* between Max the psychoanalyst and a man suitably named Thomas More. After a sexual encounter with Lola in a "kidney-shaped bunker" by the 18th green ("par 4,275 yards") of his local golf course, Tom seems troubled, and Max tries to understand what's eating him. He begins with a question:

"Didn't you tell me that your depression followed *une affaire* of the heart with a popsy at the country club?"
. . .
"Are you speaking of my fornication with Lola in number 18 bunker?"
"Fornication," repeats Max, nodding, "You see?"
"See what?"
"That you are saying that lovemaking is not a natural activity, like eating and drinking."
"No, I didn't say it wasn't natural."
"But sinful and guilt-laden."
"Not guilt-laden."
"Then sinful?"
"Only between persons not married to each other."
"I am trying to see it as you see it."
"I know you are."
"If it is sinful, why do you do it?"
"It is a great pleasure."
"I understand. Then, since it is 'sinful,' guilt feelings follow, even though it is a pleasure."
"No, they don't follow."

"Then what worries you, if you don't feel guilty?"

"That's what worries me: not feeling guilty."

"Why does that worry you?"

"Because if I felt guilty, I could get rid of it."

"How?"

"By the sacrament of penance."

"I'm trying to see it as you see it."

"I know you are."

"What I don't see is that if there is no guilt after *une affaire,* what is the problem?"

"The problem is that if there is no guilt, contrition, and a purpose of amendment, the sin cannot be forgiven."

"What does that mean, operationally speaking?"

"It means that you don't have life in you."

"Life?"

"Yes."

. . .

"In any case, your depression and suicide attempt did follow your uh 'sin.'"

"That wasn't why I was depressed."

"Why were you depressed?"

"It was Christmas Eve and there I was watching Perry Como."

"You're blocking me."

"Yes."

"What does 'purpose of amendment' mean?"

"Promising to try not to do it again and meaning it."

"And you don't intend to do that?"

"No."

"Why not, if you believe it is sinful?"

"Because it is a great pleasure."

"I don't follow."

"I know."

. . .

"If you would come back and get in the Skinner box, we could straighten it out."

"The Skinner box wouldn't help."

"We could condition away the contradiction. You'd never feel guilt."

"Then I'd really be up the creek."

"I'm trying to see it."

"I know you are."[25]

This dialogue is composed with perfect pitch. It brings together a modern man (Max), for whom pleasure without guilt is the essence of the good life, with an anachronistic man (Tom), who has dropped into the modern world as if through a time warp—a lapsed believer who still has a vestigial sense that there may be something beyond his own sensations from which he is cut off at peril to his soul. But, alarmed that he does not *feel* the distance between himself and that ungraspable phantom of something larger than himself, he fears that the practices ("contrition," "purpose of amendment") he once thought necessary for what he calls "life" no longer inspire love or awe within himself. He fears, in other words, that he is lost to God. The guilt he no longer feels had been his last reassurance that there exists something in the world that transcends himself.

When he wrote that dialogue in 1970, Walker Percy thought that Americans were looking not to guilt, but—fruitlessly—to guiltless sexual pleasure for their last link to the feeling of transcendence. Sex had become the last "sacrament of the dispossessed."[26] Thirty years later we find ourselves "engulfed in a haze of quasi-pornographic images,"[27] and the efficacy of the sacrament is in doubt.

Can anyone today really say whether *The Joy of Sex* is a parody of *The Joy of Cooking* or a straightforward recipe book for the bedroom? What about the recent advice book for men called *The Code,* which is—or is it?—a sendup of a bestselling mating manual for women called *The Rules,* which may or may not have been a spoof of itself? "We have found," say the authors of *The Code* (earnestly? flippantly?), "that superior fellatio makes us whole again; it is sex's *ne plus ultra,* a joyous return to the mythical days when the phallus was a scepter of ultimate power, an enchanted wand, a staff of life."[28] Is this an ingenuous exultation by a devotee of D. H. Lawrence or Robert Bly? Or is it a joke? And if it is a joke, on whom is it being played?

On all of us, it would seem—and the joke is getting old. As the young critic Adam Kirsch points out, "We value sexual desire so highly that we do not want it to refer beyond itself." And so we are left with no way of organizing desire into a structure of meaning. "Love in the soul is like touching in the body," one of the severest Puritan ministers was able to say, invoking an analogy at least as old as Plato's *Symposium*. Today, this capacity to turn physical pleasure into a metaphor of something more enduring—to reach for something beyond the neurological effects of vascular congestion in the genitals—seems lost to us.[29]

THE HISTORY of hope I have tried to sketch in this book is one of diminution. At first, the self expanded toward (and was sometimes overwhelmed by) the vastness of God. From the early republic to the Great Society, it remained implicated in a national ideal lesser than God but larger and more enduring than any individual citizen. Today, hope has narrowed to the vanishing point of the self alone.

This culture in which hope shrinks to the scale of self-pampering was anticipated by Thorstein Veblen a century ago in *The Theory of the Leisure Class* (1899), a book not often cited these days by American academics, who tend to prefer the cognate formulations of later European social theorists. One may choose one's authorities, but the point remains the same. The émigré philosopher Theodor Adorno, for instance, writing in the dark year of 1938, recognized that in modern culture the "pretense of individualism . . . increases in proportion to the liquidation of the individual"—by which he meant that the modern self tries to compensate with posturing and competitive self-display as it feels itself more and more cut off from anything substantial or enduring. It breaks down under bombardment by images that merge fantasy with reality, or by advertising that becomes news. In such a world it is impossible to distinguish foreground from background or the spurious from the authentic. It is a world where music becomes Muzak, where one walks into the Whitney Museum to encounter a painting by Edward Hopper hanging side by side with the latest production in what one recent writer calls the "CacaPeepee" style.[30]

A plainspeaking American moralist, Dwight Macdonald, borrowed from and abbreviated Adorno's argument into the term "masscult," which he found exemplified, in 1960, in the quintessentially American *Life Magazine*. "Nine color pages of Renoir paintings," he wrote, are "followed by a picture of a roller-skating horse . . . Just think, nine pages of Renoirs! But that roller-skating horse comes along, and the final impression is that Renoir is talented, but so is the horse." Macdonald was writing during the first phase of the television age, but we would be hard-pressed to find a better description of our own time, when discrimination is always a bad word, and when, as Lewis Lapham has put it, "the press draws no invidious distinctions between the . . . policies of the president's penis and the threat of nuclear annihilation."[31]

All these writers are latter-day Tocquevilleans. What they are talking about is the disappearance of judgment, the absorption of the reflective self (the "temperate" mind that Jefferson thought indispensable to democracy) into unconscious conformity with other interchangeable products of the marketplace. Their theme is a reprise of the contrapuntal theme of Tocqueville's great book—the somnolent likemindedness that takes hold of the mass "even under the shadow of the sovereignty of the people."[32]

For me, this power of consumer culture to evacuate the self came home vividly a few years ago when my son was twelve years old and he and his classmates were beginning the process of selecting high schools to which to apply. Parents and children met one evening under the supervision of a well-intentioned teacher who tried out an analogy she thought would get the kids thinking about how to choose the right school. "When you go into a shoe store," she said, "and you try on lots of different sneakers, how do you decide which pair is best for you?" "You take the one that fits" was, of course, the answer she was looking for—but the children had a more savvy reply. Without a flicker of irony, they sang it out in unison: *Brand name!*

In its forced consumption of masscult, the modern self becomes all and nothing at the same time, and Tocqueville's free individual, which he considered

America's gift to the world, becomes the creature he so presciently described—marooned in a perpetual present, playing alone with its trinkets and baubles. It is especially disheartening to see this process far advanced in a child.

And what does the plenty avail us? I do not know whether to trust the epidemiological studies that show rates of depression rising among Americans born in the boom years since the Second World War. I do not know if the affluent author of a recent harrowing essay about his own depression is precisely right when he calculates that "by the year 2020 depression could claim more years [of useful life] than war and AIDS put together."[33] But Tocqueville's detection of a "strange melancholy in the midst of abundance" has a special salience today—because while we have gotten very good at deconstructing old stories (the religion that was the subject of my first chapter was one such story; the nationalism that was the subject of the second chapter was another), when it comes to telling new ones, we are blocked.

An emblematic case was the fiasco at the Air and Space Museum four years ago, when the Smithsonian curators tried to mount a show to mark the fiftieth anniversary of the dropping of the atom bomb on Japan. The curators wanted to acknowledge the thousands of Japanese civilians incinerated by the bomb and the many more who died a slow death from its effects. But veterans groups wanted to highlight the salvation of American G.I.'s from what would have been an unimaginably bloody invasion of the Japanese mainland. In the end, both interpretations collapsed under irreconcilable pressures; and the fuselage of the *Enola Gay*—the plane that dropped the bomb—was hung from the ceiling as a silent relic of sheet metal and rivets. Plane and crew, the museum director later explained, were thereby allowed "to speak for themselves." The trouble is, as Richard Rorty has said in another context, that "the world does not speak. Only we do." In this case, there was no we—only the many I's who came looking for a story about the past but found themselves standing under a voiceless airplane.[34]

Here we arrive at the root of our postmodern melancholy. We live in an age of unprecedented wealth, but in the realm of narrative and symbol, we are deprived. And so the ache for meaning goes unrelieved. "The short space of sixty years," as Tocqueville put it, "can never shut in the whole of man's imagination; the incomplete joys of this world will never satisfy his heart."[35] The extra decade or two of life expectancy that we have tacked onto Tocqueville's projection does not vitiate his point.

SOMETHING, in other words, has snapped in what Jefferson called the "bands" that once connected us to one another. Even the editors of the normally cool and se-

rene *New York Times Magazine* seem to think so—as
attested by their 1998 election issue, whose cover was
emblazoned with a new preamble to the Declaration of
Independence, in mock eighteenth-century cursive let-
tering on a *faux* parchment background:

> We, the relatively unbothered and well off, hold these
> truths to be self-evident: that Big Government, Big
> Deficits and Big Tobacco are bad, but that big bath-
> rooms and 4-by-4's are not; that American overseas
> involvement should be restricted to trade agreements,
> mutual funds and the visiting of certain beachfront
> resorts; that markets can take care of themselves as
> long as they take care of us; that an individual's sex life
> is nobody's business, though highly entertaining; and
> that the only rights that really matter are those which
> indulge the Self.[36]

To be sure, there is a sense in which this culture of
self-indulgence, gently chided here in a magazine
brimming with *luxe* advertisements for props with
which to furnish the "good" life, marks the fulfillment
for huge numbers of Americans of Lincoln's dream of
prosperity. But, in a paradox that Tocqueville grasped
long ago, the cost of possessive individualism can be
the loss of the nation itself:

> I seek to trace the novel features under which despot-
> ism may appear in the world. The first thing that
> strikes the observation is an innumerable multitude of

men, all equal and alike, incessantly endeavoring to procure the petty and paltry pleasures with which they glut their lives. Each of them, living apart, is as a stranger to the fate of all the rest; his children and his private friends constitute to him the whole of mankind. As for the rest of his fellow citizens, he is close to them, but does not see them; he touches them, but he does not feel them; he exists only in himself and for himself alone; and if his kindred still remain to him, he may be said at any rate to have lost his country.[37]

Lincoln never disconnected his ideal of competitive individualism under protection of the Union from the demand that each citizen bear some measure of responsibility for his fellows. Everything he wrote about the rights of the self (culminating in the Second Inaugural Address) was inflected by a sense of public responsibility; and, of everything he believed, his deepest belief was that to save the Union meant to enlarge the circle of hope.

But who looks today to the widening of the circle? In my city, the city of Whitman (who once remarked that "the true gravitation-hold of liberalism in the United States will be a more universal ownership of property, general homesteads, general comfort—a vast, intertwining reticulation of wealth"),[38] the stretch limos take up two and three parking spaces at a time while the homeless, plentiful as pigeons, beg a quarter for wiping the windshields. The persistence of poverty

in the United States has never been more striking—
not because it is a new problem, but because, by the
principle of contrast, it is more glaring than at any
time since the Gilded Age. We treat the poor as if they
were beggars shuffling outside a restaurant, to whom
we toss a coin on the way in, in the hope that they will
be gone by the time we go home. We mutter about
their laziness (if we are on the right), or talk of their
misfortune and mistreatment (if we are on the left); but
for them the difference between right and left has become purely rhetorical.

What does this mean for our collective future? Despite my earlier remarks about the limited value of
numbers for thinking about past and present, let me
mention some figures that should, at the least, disturb
us. Students at our flagship public university, the City
University of New York, once the portal of entry into
the culture of hope for children of immigrants drawn
from a functional public school system, now have a
four-year graduation rate of less than 10 percent and
combined SAT scores averaging in the 700s. One third
of these students have children of their own, many
illegitimate, without fathers willing to acknowledge
them—a situation that Daniel Patrick Moynihan calls
"a volcanic change in family structure, for which there
is no comparable experience in human history."[39] Sena-
tor Moynihan may magnify the problem, but he does
not fundamentally distort it. Growing up without ex-

emplars of self-discipline, without fluency in the ways of the larger culture or the skills requisite for success in the modern marketplace, how dare these children harbor hope for the future? And what of the more than two million American adults in prison—a figure almost ten times higher than thirty years ago? What chance have they to become the Tocquevillean citizens upon whom democracy depends?

From the comfort of the academy, we look at our past and are quick to say that a culture with too little freedom and too much brutality was a bad culture. But do we have the nerve to say of ourselves that a culture locked in a soul-starving present, in which the highest aspiration—for those who can afford to try—is to keep the body forever young, is no culture at all?

BEFORE bringing this jeremiad to an end, I want to make a few retrospective remarks. First of all, there is much to be said against any scheme of periodization, including my own too-neat division of American history into two phases of coherent belief followed by a third phase of incoherence and nervous waiting. In the first period, Christians seldom agreed on what, exactly, Christianity meant. In the second period, violent conflict was commonplace over the nature and extent of citizenship rights. And the boundary between the two phases—between Christian symbology and the civil religion—was never as sharp as I have drawn it.

It should also be said that the civil religion may not be entirely dead today, but may be evolving into what the sociologist Alan Wolfe calls "mature patriotism"— a love of country free of idolatry and "leavened with realism."[40] There is a phrase in Antonio Gramsci's *Prison Notebooks* that strikes me in this connection as a useful way of thinking about the life cycle of ideas—a geological metaphor by which Gramsci represents the time-lag between the appearance of new ideas and the disappearance of old ones. "All previous philosophy," he says, leaves "stratified deposits in popular philosophy."[41] The deposited ideas of Christianity and civil religion are still the bedrock of our culture, whatever intellectuals may think of them. And the history of ideas is usually better understood as a process of incorporation and transformation than as a series of successive movements discrete and distinct from one another.

It is also possible that the structure of human desire itself may be undergoing evolution. Much of what I have said about melancholy is based on the premise, as Melville expressed it, that "we become sad in the first place because we have nothing stirring to do." But some would argue that the yearning one hears in this remark—the need to force the world to yield to one's will—is a specifically male, and entirely dispensable, form of desire. Some evolutionary psychologists (formerly known as sociobiologists) even think that survival of the species requires that this form of desire be superseded by a different kind—that, in Jill Ker Con-way's words, "service motivations replace erotic pas-sions as the governing force in life."[42]

As for the persistent desire for money—which shows no sign of abatement—much of what I have said ech-oes Tocqueville, who had an aristocrat's distaste for the "petty and paltry" pleasures of the *arriviste*. Neither his brilliance nor his prescience should deflect us from the fact that the drive for money—especially by those not born with it—has always been a creative as well as a corrosive force in American life. Still, I think we are entitled, indeed obliged, to wonder whether in all our history there has ever been such a frenzy for money on such a scale as there is today.

Finally, there are more reasons to be hopeful than might seem to be registered in my narrative of declen-sion. For one thing, the sense of fairness and decency for which the American people are regularly compli-mented by their politicians is actually real and abiding. Against all odds, the live issues of our day are still sometimes debated with dignity; whatever position one takes in the debate over affirmative action, for in-stance, it has often been a debate over how the princi-ple of fairness should be applied rather than over raw group interests. Whatever one thinks of gay marriage, or gays in the military, or the question of nature vs. nurture in determining gay sexuality, homophobia in the United States has markedly subsided since the devastation of AIDS. And whatever one may think of the current president and his enemies, the public struck a good balance during his humiliation in expressing disgust both with him and with the prosecutor and press, who relentlessly exposed his private behavior.

Yet, despite all these plausible qualifications of what I have said (and more could be adduced), I stand by my claim that the most striking feature of contemporary culture is the unslaked craving for transcendence. To this claim, it might be objected that we are witnessing resurgent orthodoxy among Christians, Jews, and Muslims in the United States, as well as the proliferation of New Age and other support groups—Promise-Keepers, Channelers, self-segregated groups expressing ethnic or gender solidarity, reading groups, recovery groups, and innumerable other voluntary associations of the sort Tocqueville recognized long ago as a peculiarly American phenomenon.

But Tocqueville understood the voluntary groupings of his time as complementary to a combination of reverence and intimate affection that Americans felt toward the nation that freed them to choose their personal affiliations. For many people today, voluntary associations can doubtless still be soul-saving; but they tend to express a turn inward away from public engagement. They are clubbish and resolutely local, and unlikely to lead outward toward a sense of connection with an overarching human community. How many times have we heard—and how often have those of us who are teachers seen confirmed—that the best and brightest young people turn away from public service toward private enterprise? The imagination of the young may still be drawn toward what one Puritan writer called "an *Aliquid Ultra,* something further to be sought after, besides what we have found in ourselves"—but our symbols for this "something further" are terribly weakened.[43]

This sapping of symbolic power from transcendent ideas such as God and nation cannot, in the end, be replenished by intensified local commitments—because the most urgent problems of our time are not local problems. We have a global marketplace, but the meager regulatory institutions we have developed (United Nations, World Bank, World Court, International Monetary Fund) have nothing like the power they need to moderate the turbulence of the market or to check the cruelties of local political regimes. From time to time we are embarrassed to be reminded that our gym shoes are made in sweatshops by Asian children, or that our tobacco companies, a bit more hampered than they used to be at home, are free, and zealous, to export cancer abroad. But embarrassment, alas, has no efficacy.

John Dewey saw the problem of post-nationalism as early as the 1920s—a time of market frenzy and international disorder not dissimilar to our own—when he wrote that "symbols control sentiment and thought, and the new age has no symbols consonant with its activities."[44] To someone of my family origin, this kind of discordance has a frightening aspect because it suggests that some new cult or *Reich* may be advancing upon us to fill the yearning for something grand, something stirring. I speak now personally, as the child of German Jewish parents who fled to America from a country whose own long-deferred *Sehnsucht* was satisfied only when a German Satan installed himself as emperor over a German-made hell on earth. I am not proposing the usual facile parallel between the Weimar Republic and our own perilous times. I do not think some new beast is slouching toward America to be born. But *something* new is coming. Tocqueville explains why it must, and why it will:

> Religion . . . is only one particular form of hope, and it is as natural to the human heart as hope itself. It is by a sort of intellectual aberration, and in a way, by doing moral violence to their own nature, that men detach themselves from religious beliefs; an invincible inclination draws them back. Incredulity is an accident; faith is the only permanent state of mankind.[45]

According to this axiom, the question is never whether some kind of faith will reemerge. The question is, what will it be?

Virtually everyone who thinks seriously about the

human future contemplates a time—some with hope, some with dread—when human beings will no longer construct their identities within the symbolic and functional structure of the nation-state. Just before the outbreak of the last great imperial war, the journalist Clarence Streidt published a bestselling book with the Lincolnian title *Union Now* (1939), in which he called for a world federation to which individual states would cede certain powers for the sake of the whole. If we are still waiting, it is in part because, as Christopher Lasch once described the problem, "the capacity for loyalty is stretched too thin when it tries to attach itself to the hypothetical solidarity of the whole human race. It needs to attach itself to specific people and places, not to an abstract ideal of universal human rights"—especially, one might add, when human rights, even in the limited sense of equal opportunity, are still imperiled at home.[46]

If and when these rights are someday secured for all Americans, the American dream will not have been fulfilled. It has always been a global dream. A phrase from Witold Gombrowicsz expresses the aspiration succinctly: "To be really French means to see something beyond France."[47] To be really American has always meant to see something beyond America. This is what the Puritans meant in insisting that if we fail to contribute to some good beyond ourselves, we condemn ourselves to the hell of loneliness. It is what

Lincoln meant when he insisted that the rights of each person depend on the rights of all persons.

Let me close by recalling that when Emerson felt his fathers' version of Christianity ebbing in the 1830s he tried to discern whether a new faith was coming, and what it might be. He got it right, I think, when he gave up the effort, saying, "all attempts to project and establish a Cultus with new rites and forms, seem to me in vain. Faith makes us, and not we it, and faith makes its own forms." Meanwhile, he added, in a wonderfully Emersonian contradiction, "let us do what we can to rekindle the smouldering nigh quenched fire on the altar."[48]

For those of us engaged as teachers and writers with the history and literature of the United States, I can think of no more noble charge while we wait.

Notes · Index

Notes

PROLOGUE

1. Clifford Geertz, "Religion as a Cultural System," in Geertz, *The Interpretation of Cultures* (New York: Basic Books, 1973), pp. 99, 102.

2. Burton, quoted in Wolf Lepenies, *Melancholy and Society* (Cambridge, Mass.: Harvard University Press, 1992), p. 15; Thomas Hooker, *The Poor Doubting Christian Drawn unto Christ* (1629), in *Thomas Hooker: Writings in England and Holland, 1626–1633,* ed. George H. Williams et al. (Cambridge, Mass.: Harvard University Press, 1975), p. 157.

3. Alexis de Tocqueville, *Democracy in America,* trans. Phillips Bradley (New York: Vintage, 1990), 2 vols., 2: 138–139.

4. Alexis de Tocqueville, *Democracy in America* (New York: Harper, 1988), trans. George Lawrence, p. 296. (I have used both the Bradley and Lawrence editions; future citations are indicated by the translator's name.)

5. Edmund S. Morgan, ed., *The Diary of Michael Wigglesworth, 1653–1657* (New York: Harper, 1965), p. 8.

6. Ralph Waldo Emerson, "Experience" (1844), in Stephen E. Whicher, ed., *Selections from Ralph Waldo Emerson: An Organic Anthology* (Boston: Houghton Mifflin, 1957), pp. 254–255.

7. Michael Oakeshott, "Political Education," in Oakeshott, *Rationalism in Politics and Other Essays* (Indianapolis: Liberty Press, 1991), p. 48.

8. Conor Cruise O'Brien, *God Land: Reflections on Religion and Nationalism* (Cambridge, Mass.: Harvard University Press, 1988), p. 49.

9. William James, *The Varieties of Religious Experience* (1903), in Bruce Kuklick, ed., *William James: Writings, 1902–1910* (New York: Library of America, 1987), p. 250.

10. R. G. Collingwood, *The Idea of History* (Oxford: Oxford University Press, 1956), p. 213.

11. Norman Mailer, *The Armies of the Night* (New York: New American Library, 1968), p. 255.

12. Walt Whitman, *Democratic Vistas* (1870), in Justin Kaplan, ed., *Walt Whitman: Complete Poetry and Collected Prose* (New York: Library of America, 1982), p. 944. Iver Bernstein, in *The New York City Draft Riots* (New York: Oxford University Press, 1990), gives a vivid account of anti-black violence during the unrest.

13. William James, *Pragmatism* (1907; New York: New American Library, 1955), p. 140.

14. Richard Hofstadter, *The American Political Tradition* (New York: Knopf, 1948), p. 132.

15. Thomas Jefferson, *Notes on the State of Virginia* (1781), in Merrill Peterson, ed., *The Portable Jefferson* (New York: Vi-

king, 1975), p. 187; W. E. B. Du Bois, "The Concept of Race" (1940), in Eric Sundquist, ed., *The Oxford W. E. B. Du Bois Reader* (New York: Oxford University Press, 1996), p. 77.

16. Emerson, "Circles" (1840), in Whicher, ed., *Selections from Emerson*, p. 169.

1. GOD

1. Alan Taylor, "In a Strange Way," review of Jill Lepore, *The Name of War: King Philip's War and the Origins of American Identity, New Republic*, April 13, 1998, 37; Tocqueville, *Democracy in America*, trans. Bradley, 1: 29.

2. Perry Miller, "Religion and Society in the Early Literature of Virginia," in Miller, *Errand into the Wilderness* (Cambridge, Mass.: Harvard University Press, 1956), pp. 101, 117; Jon Butler, *Awash in a Sea of Faith: Christianizing the American People* (Cambridge, Mass.: Harvard University Press, 1990), p. 42.

3. On the origin of the term "Puritan," see Patrick Collinson, *The Elizabethan Puritan Movement* (Los Angeles: University of California Press, 1967), pp. 22–28.

4. John Brinsely, *The Preacher's Charge and People's Duty* (London, 1631), p. 4.

5. Richard Hooker, *Of the Laws of Ecclesiastical Polity* (1593–1597; London: J. M. Dent, 1907), 2 vols., 1: 229 (bk. 1, sect. xvi, topic 6).

6. Tocqueville, *Democracy in America*, trans. Bradley, 1: 31; "A Puritan . . . heart," quoted in Patrick Collinson, "A Comment: Concerning the Name Puritan," *Journal of Ecclesiastical History* 31, no. 4 (1980), 487; D. H. Lawrence, *Studies*

in Classic American Literature (1923; New York: Viking, 1964), p. 3; William Carlos Williams, *In the American Grain* (1925; New York: New Directions, 1956), p. 63.

7. Winthrop, letter to his wife, in Edmund S. Morgan, ed., *The Founding of Massachusetts* (Indianapolis: Bobbs-Merrill, 1964), p. 286.

8. Thomas Hooker, *The Soules Preparation for Salvation* (London, 1628), p. 42; John Winthrop, *A Model of Christian Charity,* in Alan Heimert and Andrew Delbanco, eds., *The Puritans in America* (Cambridge, Mass.: Harvard University Press, 1985), p. 88.

9. Thomas Shepard, *The Sincere Convert* (ca. 1635), in John Albro, ed., *The Works of Thomas Shepard* (Boston, 1853), 3 vols., 1: 35; Jonathan Edwards, *Sinners in the Hands of an Angry God* (1741), in John E. Smith, Harry S. Stout, and Kenneth P. Minkema, eds., *A Jonathan Edwards Reader* (New Haven: Yale University Press, 1995), p. 98.

10. Gerald McDonald, ed., *Poems of Stephen Crane* (New York: Thomas Y. Crowell, 1964), p. 49.

11. John Cotton, *A Treatise of the Covenant of Grace* (1636), in Heimert and Delbanco, eds., *The Puritans in America,* p. 151.

12. Thomas Gataker, *On the Nature and Use of Lots* (London, 1619), p. 17; Cotton Mather, *Magnalia Christi Americana,* Books I and II, ed. Kenneth B. Murdock (Cambridge, Mass.: Harvard University Press, 1977), p. 97; "The Lynn End 'Earthquake' Relations of 1727," ed. Kenneth P. Minkema, *New England Quarterly* 69 (1996), 483. The richest account of lay piety in early New England is David D. Hall, *Worlds of Wonder, Days of Judgment* (New York: Knopf, 1989).

13. *New York Magazine,* March 9, 1998, p. 16.

14. Richard Sibbes, *The Bruised Reed and Smoking Flax* (London, 1630), p. 43; William James, *Varieties of Religious Experience,* p. 191.

15. Cotton Mather, *Magnalia Christi Americana,* p. 109.

16. Harry Stout, *The New England Soul* (New York: Oxford University Press, 1986), p. 4.

17. John Cotton, *A Brief Exposition of the Whole Book of Canticles, or, Song of Solomon* (London, 1642), p. 179.

18. William James, *Varieties of Religious Experience,* p. 211; Sibbes, *Bruised Reed,* p. 108; Thomas Hooker, *The Application of Redemption, the Ninth and Tenth Books* (London, 1659), pp. 363–364.

19. George H. Williams, "Called by Thy Name, Leave us Not: The Case of Mrs. Joan Drake, a Formative Episode in the Pastoral Career of Thomas Hooker in England," *Harvard Library Bulletin* 14, no. 2 (April 1968), 116–117.

20. John Winthrop, *Journal,* ed. James Kendall Hosmer (New York: Scribner, 1908), 2 vols., 1: 220.

21. William Perkins, *Works* (London, 1608–1609), 3 vols., 1: 3.

22. Jonathan Edwards, *The Nature of True Virtue* (1758), ed. William K. Frankena (Ann Arbor: University of Michigan Press, 1960), p. 61.

23. Edwards, *Personal Narrative,* in Smith et al., eds., *Jonathan Edwards Reader,* p. 285.

24. Hooker, *Application of Redemption,* p. 150; John Cotton, *The Way of Life* (London, 1641), p. 280; Jonathan Edwards, *A Treatise Concerning Religious Affections* (1746; New Haven: Yale University Press, 1959), p. 173.

25. John Cotton, *Christ the Fountaine of Life* (London, 1651),

p. 16; Emerson, *Nature* (1836), in Whicher, ed., *Selections from Emerson,* p. 23; Van Wyck Brooks, *America's Coming-of-Age* (1915; New York: Anchor, 1958), p. 11.

26. Davenport, quoted in Anne S. Brown and David D. Hall, "Family Strategies and Religious Practice: Baptism and the Lord's Supper in Early New England," in David D. Hall, ed., *Lived Religion in America* (Princeton: Princeton University Press, 1997), p. 46; John Cotton, *A Treatise of the Covenant of Grace* (London, 1671), p. 204.

27. Cotton, *Christ the Fountaine,* p. 200.

28. William James, *Varieties of Religious Experience,* p. 219.

29. Ibid.; Edwards, *Treatise Concerning Religious Affections,* pp. 411, 441.

30. Winthrop, *Model of Christian Charity,* in Heimert and Delbanco, *Puritans in America,* p. 88; Winthrop, letter to his wife, in Morgan, ed., *Founding of Massachusetts,* p. 186; *Paradise Lost,* bk. IX, ll. 955–959.

31. John Cotton, *The Way of Life* (London, 1641), p. 84.

32. Winthrop, *Journal,* 1: 276; Cotton Mather, *Magnalia Christi Americana,* p. 147; Robert Calef, *More Wonders of the Invisible World* (1700), in George Lincoln Burr, ed., *Narratives of the Witchcraft Cases, 1648–1706* (New York: Scribner, 1914), p. 325.

33. M. Halsey Thomas, ed., *The Diary of Samuel Sewall* (New York: Farrar, Straus and Giroux, 1973), 2 vols., 2: 731 (Oct.25, 1713).

34. Louis B. Wright and Marion Tinling, eds., *The Great American Gentleman: The Secret Diary of William Byrd of Westover, 1709–1712* (New York: G. P. Putnam's Sons, 1963), p. 73 (April 21, 1710).

35. Robert Beverley, *The History and Present State of Virginia*

(1705; Charlottesville: University of Virginia Press, 1968), p. 16.

36. William Ellery Channing, *Works* (Boston, 1848), 6 vols., 1: 220.

37. John Cotton, *A Briefe Exposition with Practicall Observations upon the Whole Book of Ecclesiastes* (London, 1657), p. 195.

38. Emerson, *Address to the Graduating Class of the Harvard Divinity School* (1838), in Whicher, ed., *Selections from Emerson,* p. 111.

2. NATION

1. Emerson, *Divinity School Address,* in Whicher, ed., *Selections from Emerson,* pp. 108–109; on the antebellum growth of religious institutions, see Butler, *Awash in a Sea of Faith,* esp. p. 270.

2. Emerson, *Divinity School Address,* in Whicher, ed., *Selections from Emerson,* p. 111; Tocqueville, *Democracy in America,* trans. Lawrence, pp. 295, 293; Philip Schaff, *America: A Sketch of Its Political, Social, and Religious Character* (1855; Cambridge, Mass.: Harvard University Press, 1961), p. 76; Frances Trollope, *Domestic Manners of the Americans* (1832; New York: Knopf, 1949), p. 75. Lewis O. Saum, *The Popular Mood of America, 1860–1890* (Lincoln: University of Nebraska Press, 1990), p. 69, argues that Emerson made his "dark assessment" about the state of religion "too soon," but that "had he waited thirty or forty years he would have been describing the common people, as well as the elevated among whom he moved."

3. Butler, *Awash in a Sea of Faith,* p. 263.

4. Richard John, *Spreading the News: The American Postal Sys-*

tem from Franklin to Morse (Cambridge, Mass.: Harvard University Press, 1995), p. 169. "Amicable separation" is Schaff's phrase; *America,* p. 76.

5. Schaff, *America,* p. 96; Melville, *Pierre; or, The Ambiguities* (1852; Evanston: Northwestern University Press, 1971), p. 273; Oneida song quoted in Mark Holloway, *Heavens on Earth: Utopian Communities in America, 1680–1880* (New York: Dover, 1966), p. 179; Joel Porte, ed., *Emerson in His Journals* (Cambridge, Mass.: Harvard University Press, 1982), p. 63 (March 1, 1827).

6. Emerson, *Divinity School Address,* in Whicher, ed., *Selections from Emerson,* pp. 107, 105. See Jerry Wayne Brown, *The Rise of Biblical Criticism in America, 1800–1870* (Middletown, Conn.: Wesleyan University Press, 1969), pp. 140–152.

7. Porte, *Emerson in His Journals,* p. 197.

8. Whitman, "Preface" (1855) to *Leaves of Grass,* in Kaplan, ed., *Whitman: Complete Poetry and Collected Prose,* p. 5.

9. Whitman, *Democratic Vistas,* in Kaplan, ed., *Whitman: Complete Poetry and Collected Prose,* p. 952; Tocqueville, *Democracy in America,* trans. Lawrence, p. 237.

10. William James, *Varieties of Religious Experience,* p. 249; Tocqueville, *Democracy in America,* trans. Bradley, 1: 61.

11. Edward Everett Hale, *The Man Without a Country and Other Stories* (Boston, 1899), p. 50.

12. Whitman, *Democratic Vistas,* in Kaplan, ed., *Whitman: Complete Poetry and Collected Prose,* p. 955. The best account of the business conditions under which American authors worked remains William Charvat's *Literary Publishing in America: 1790–1850* (Philadelphia: University of Pennsyl-

vania Press, 1959): "When a publisher reprinted a foreign work at his own risk, he divided what would have been the author's profit with his retailers in the form of high discounts, which encouraged the retailers to push sales. But the small discount which the retailer received on a copyrighted native work was no inducement to salesmanship" (p. 42).

13. Whitman, *Song of Myself,* in Kaplan ed., *Whitman: Complete Poetry and Collected Prose,* pp. 200–201.

14. Melville, *Moby-Dick,* ch. 14.

15. Tocqueville, *Democracy in America,* trans. Bradley, 2: 62, 72.

16. Whitman, *Democratic Vistas,* in Kaplan, ed., *Whitman: Complete Poetry and Collected Prose,* pp. 949, 981; Melville to Hawthorne, Nov. [17?], 1851, in *Correspondence of Herman Melville,* ed. Lynn Horth (Evanston: Northwestern University Press, 1993), p. 212; Edward Johnson, *The Wonder-Working Providence of Sion's Saviour in New England* (1653), ed. J. Franklin Jameson (New York: Scribner, 1910), p. 49.

17. Melville, *White-Jacket; or, The World in a Man-of-War* (1850), ch. 36.

18. Brownson, quoted in Nelson W. Aldrich Jr., *Old Money: The Mythology of America's Upper Class* (New York: Vintage, 1988), p. 38.

19. Abraham Lincoln, *Speech on the Sub-Treasury at Springfield, Illinois* (Dec. 26, 1839), in Don E. Fehrenbacher, ed., *Abraham Lincoln: Speeches and Writings* (New York: Library of America, 1989), 2 vols., 1: 65.

20. Schaff, *America,* p. 88; Ebeneezer Frothingham, *Articles of*

Faith and Practice (Newport, 1750), p. 370; Melville, *Moby-Dick* (1851), ch. 26.

21. Tocqueville, *Democracy in America,* trans. Bradley, 2: 53; *Democracy in America,* trans. Lawrence, pp. 94–95.

22. Schaff, *America,* pp. 37–38; Jefferson, *Notes on the State of Virginia,* p. 125.

23. Jefferson, *Notes on the State of Virginia,* p. 125.

24. *Federalist Papers,* nos. 2 and 14.

25. Hannah Arendt, *The Origins of Totalitarianism* (New York: Harcourt, Brace, 1976), p. 161.

26. Jefferson, *Notes on the State of Virginia,* p. 181.

27. Schaff, *America,* p. 87; Tocqueville, *Democracy in America,* trans. Lawrence, p. 238. Italics added.

28. John Clive, *Not by Fact Alone: Essays on the Writing and Reading of History* (Boston: Houghton Mifflin, 1989), p. 253.

29. For a valuable account of one immigrant group's crossing of the "color" line, see Noel Ignatiev, *How the Irish Became White* (New York: Routledge, 1995).

30. Melville, *Moby-Dick,* ch. 16.

31. Melville, *Moby-Dick,* ch. 27.

32. Jefferson, *Notes on the State of Virginia,* p. 217; Frederick Douglass, "What to the Slave Is the Fourth of July?" in Nina Baym et al., eds., *The Norton Anthology of American Literature,* 4th ed. (New York: Norton, 1994), p. 2003.

33. Lincoln, First Debate with Stephen Douglas (Aug. 21, 1858), in Fehrenbacher, ed., *Speeches and Writings,* 1: 514.

34. William Herndon and Albert Beveridge, quoted in Dwight Anderson, *Abraham Lincoln: The Quest for Immortality* (New York: Knopf, 1982), p. 113.

35. Lincoln, quoted in Stephen B. Oates, *With Malice Toward*

None: The Life of Abraham Lincoln (New York: New American Library, 1977), p. 108.

36. Lincoln, *Speech on Kansas-Nebraska Act* (Oct. 16, 1854), in Fehrenbacher, ed., *Speeches and Writings,* 1: 315; Samuel Johnson, quoted in John Chester Miller, *The Wolf by the Ears: Thomas Jefferson and Slavery* (New York: New American Library, 1980), p. 8.

37. Lincoln, *Speech on Dred Scott Decision* (June 26, 1857), in Fehrenbacher, ed., *Speeches and Writings,* 1: 397; Douglass, quoted in David Donald, *Lincoln* (London: Jonathan Cape, 1995), p. 221.

38. Douglass, *My Bondage and My Freedom* (1855; New York: Dover, 1969), p. 282.

39. Fehrenbacher, ed., *Lincoln: Speeches and Writings,* 1: 396–397.

40. For Lincoln's interpretation of the founders' views of slavery, see his *Address at Cooper Institute* (Feb. 27, 1860), in Fehrenbacher, ed., *Speeches and Writings,* 2: 111–130.

41. Lincoln, quoted in Robert A. Ferguson, *Law and Letters in American Culture* (Cambridge, Mass.: Harvard University Press, 1984), p. 312.

42. Lincoln, letter to Albert G. Hodges (April 4, 1864), in Fehrenbacher, ed., *Speeches and Writings,* 2: 586. Edmund Wilson argued in *Patriotic Gore: Studies in the Literature of the American Civil War* (New York: Oxford University Press, 1966), p. 108, that at an early age Lincoln "saw himself in an heroic role" and as destined "to perform a spectacular feat."

43. Lincoln, *Address to the Wisconsin Agricultural Society* (Sept. 30, 1859) and *Speech at New Haven* (March 6, 1860), in Fehrenbacher, ed., *Speeches and Writings,* 1: 97–98, 144.

44. Henry David Thoreau, *A Plea for Captain John Brown* (1859), in *Walden and Other Writings,* ed. Brooks Atkinson (New York: Modern Library, 1950), p. 704.

45. Lincoln, *Speech at Independence Hall* (Feb. 22, 1861), in Fehrenbacher, ed., *Speeches and Writings,* 2: 213.

46. Lincoln, "Fragment on Slavery," in Fehrenbacher, ed., *Speeches and Writings,* 1: 303. Lincoln's point was not new; the historian George Bancroft, for example, had compressed it, with Brahmin understatement, into a sentence years before: "Men are prone to fail in equity towards those whom their pride regards as their inferiors." But if Lincoln added nothing new in substance to American ideals, he spoke in words so stirring that he gave old thoughts a new purchase on the American imagination.

47. *Diary of Michael Wigglesworth,* p. 3; Lincoln, *Speech on Kansas-Nebraska Act* and *Second Inaugural Address* (March 4, 1865), in Fehrenbacher, ed., *Speeches and Writings,* 1: 339–340; 2: 687. For an anticipation of Lincoln's theme of blood compensation, see George Templeton Strong's remark, as quoted in George Fredrickson, *The Inner Civil War: Northern Intellectuals and the Crisis of the Union* (New York: Harper, 1968), p. 103, that "without the shedding of blood there is no remission of sins."

48. Thoreau, *Walden,* p. 9; Douglass, *My Bondage and My Freedom,* p. 273.

49. Stephens, quoted in Wilson, *Patriotic Gore,* p. 99.

50. Lincoln, *Speech at Chicago, Illinois* (July 10, 1858), in Fehrenbacher, ed., *Speeches and Writings,* 1: 456.

51. Joseph P. Thompson, *Abraham Lincoln; His Life and its Lessons. A Sermon Preached on Sabbath, April 30, 1865,* in Frank Freidel, ed., *Union Pamphlets of the Civil War* (Cam-

bridge, Mass.: Harvard University Press, 1967), 2 vols., 2: 1179.

3. SELF

1. William Bradford, *Of Plymouth Plantation* (w. 1630–1650; New York: Modern Library, 1952), p. 61; John Cotton, *A Briefe Exposition upon Ecclesiastes,* p. 120.

2. Henry Adams, *The Education of Henry Adams* (1907; Boston: Houghton Mifflin, 1973), p. 266; Emerson, *Historic Notes of Life and Letters in New England* (1880), in *The American Transcendentalists,* ed. Perry Miller (New York: Anchor, 1957), pp. 5–6. Robert Putnam's widely noted essay "Bowling Alone: America's Declining Social Capital" was published in the *Journal of Democracy* 1 (Jan. 1995). For a shrewd critique of its implication that civil society is failing, see Nicholas Lemann, "Kicking in Groups," *Atlantic Monthly* 277 (April 1996), 22–26.

3. Gore Vidal, *Screening History* (Cambridge, Mass.: Harvard University Press, 1992), p. 5; William Bennett, *The De-Valuing of America* (New York: Simon and Schuster, 1994); Arthur Schlesinger Jr., *The Disuniting of America* (New York: Norton, 1992); Robert Redford, *Quiz Show* (1994); Don DeLillo, *Underworld* (New York: Scribner, 1997), p. 94.

4. T. Jackson Lears, "Looking Backward," *Lingua Franca,* Dec./Jan. 1998, 66.

5. H. C. Dodge, quoted in John Thorn, *Baseball: Our Game* (New York: Penguin, 1995), pp. 8–9.

6. Henry Louis Gates Jr., "The End of Loyalty," *New Yorker,* March 9, 1998, 34–44; William Safire, "The Death of

Outrage," *New York Times,* March 19, 1998, p. A21. Notable examples of scholarly jeremiads include Henry May, *The End of American Innocence* (New York: Knopf, 1959); Daniel Bell, *The End of Ideology* (New York: Free Press, 1962), and Francis Fukuyama, "The End of History," *National Interest* 16 (Summer 1998), 3–18.

7. Tocqueville, *Democracy in America,* trans. Bradley, 2: 212.

8. Daniel Bell, "Crime as an American Way of Life," in *The End of Ideology,* pp. 127–150.

9. Horace Kallen, "Democracy versus the Melting Pot," *The Nation,* Feb. 18, 1915, 194; Feb. 25, 1915, 220; Henry Adams, *The Education,* p. 499.

10. Thoreau, *Walden,* p. 70; Brooks, *America's Coming-of-Age,* p. 16.

11. Thucydides, *History of the Peloponnesian War,* trans. Rex Warner (London: Penguin, 1972), p. 150.

12. Edith Wharton, *The House of Mirth* (New York: Penguin, 1985), p. 111 (later in life Wharton devoted herself considerably to charitable work); John Jay Chapman, "The Unity of Human Nature," (1900), in *Unbought Spirit: A John Jay Chapman Reader,* ed. Richard Stone (Chicago: University of Chicago Press, 1998), p. 29.

13. See Ron Chernow's biography of John D. Rockefeller, *Titan* (New York: Random House, 1998), pp. 145–152, on Rockefeller's vision of "God as . . . a sort of honorary shareholder of Standard Oil," the gigantic oil trust he regarded as "the *antidote* to social Darwinism, a way to bring universal brotherhood to a fractious industry."

14. Recent examples of historians who trace the origins of the welfare state to the aftermath of the Civil War include Theda Skocpol, *Protecting Soldiers and Mothers: The Political*

Origins of Social Policy in the United States (Cambridge, Mass.: Harvard University Press, 1992); and Patrick J. Kelly, *Creating a National Home: Building the Veterans' Welfare State, 1860–1900* (Cambridge, Mass.: Harvard University Press, 1997).

15. Whitman, *Democratic Vistas,* in Kaplan, ed., *Whitman: Complete Poetry and Collected Prose,* p. 949.

16. William James, *Varieties of Religious Experience,* pp. 249–250.

17. See Herbert Parmet, *George Bush* (New York: Scribner, 1997), pp. 424–425.

18. Bill Readings, *The University in Ruins* (Cambridge, Mass.: Harvard University Press, 1996), p. 112.

19. Todd Gitlin sees the sun setting in August 1964, when the Mississippi Freedom Democratic Party was denied a seat at the Democratic convention and Congress passed the Tonkin Gulf Resolution; *The Sixties: Years of Hope, Days of Rage* (New York: Bantam, 1978), p. 178.

20. Robert Bellah, "Civil Religion in America," in Bellah, *Beyond Belief: Essays on Religion in a Post-Traditional World* (New York: Harper and Row, 1970), pp. 171, 183.

21. Whitman, *Specimen Days,* in Kaplan, ed., *Whitman: Complete Poetry and Collected Prose,* p. 718. Anyone with a taste for irony will have noted that when news broke of President Clinton's exploits with Monica Lewinsky, it was reported that he had given her a book of erotic poems, "the most sentimental gift" she ever received from him, according to Ms. Lewinsky. The book in question turned out to be a copy of *Leaves of Grass.*

22. Derek Bok, *The State of the Nation* (Cambridge, Mass.: Harvard University Press, 1996), p. 4, reports that the vast

majority of Americans in 1960 thought the country was moving nicely ahead but by the 1990s two-thirds believed it was "headed in the wrong direction."

23. *New York Times,* Jan. 27, 1939, p. 21. I owe this reference, with thanks, to Professor Robert Burt of the Yale Law School.

24. Greene, *The End of the Affair,* p. 45; Lionel Trilling, *Matthew Arnold* (New York: Columbia University Press, 1949), p. 137.

25. Walker Percy, *Love in the Ruins* (New York: Farrar, Straus and Giroux, 1971), pp. 116–118.

26. Walker Percy, *The Last Gentleman* (New York: Ballantine, 1966), p. 220. Andrew Sullivan, in *Love Undetectable: Notes on Friendship, Sex, and Survival* (New York: Knopf, 1998), pp. 195–196, speaks of eros as our new civil religion.

27. Lewis Lapham, "In the Garden of Tabloid Delight," *Harper's,* Aug. 1997, 37.

28. Ellen Fein and Sherrie Schneider, *The Rules: Time-Tested Secrets for Capturing the Heart of Mr. Right* (New York: Warner, 1995); Nate Penn and Lawrence LaRose, *The Code: Time-Tested Secrets for Getting What You Want from Women — Without Marrying Them!* (New York: Simon and Schuster, 1996), p. 105.

29. Adam Kirsch, review of Frank Bidart's *Desire, New Republic,* Oct. 27, 1997, 38; Thomas Hooker, *The Soules Effectual Calling or Vocation* (London, 1637), p. 219.

30. Adorno, in Andrew Arato and Eike Gebhardt, eds., *The Essential Frankfurt Reader* (New York: Continuum, 1982), p. 280; phrase from Mark Stevens, "Is Sex Dead," *New York Magazine,* July 21, 1997, 40.

31. Dwight Macdonald, *Against the American Grain: Essays on the Effects of Mass Culture* (London: Victor Gollancz, 1963), p. 12; Lapham, "In the Garden of Tabloid Delight," 42.

32. Tocqueville, *Democracy in America,* trans. Lawrence, p. 693.

33. Gerald L. Klerman and Myrna M. Weissman, "Increasing Rates of Depression," *Journal of the American Medical Association* 261, no. 15 (April 21, 1989), 2229–2235; Andrew Solomon, "The Anatomy of Melancholy," *New Yorker,* Jan. 12, 1998, 46.

34. The museum's director, Martin Harwit, quoted in the *Tampa Tribune,* June 25, 1996; Richard Rorty, *Contingency, Irony, and Solidarity* (Cambridge: Cambridge University Press, 1989), p. 6.

35. Tocqueville, *Democracy in America,* trans. Lawrence, p. 296.

36. *New York Times Magazine,* Nov. 1, 1998.

37. Tocqueville, *Democracy in America,* trans. Bradley, 2: 318.

38. Whitman, *Democratic Vistas,* in Kaplan, ed., *Whitman: Complete Poetry and Collected Prose,* p. 950.

39. *Report of the Mayor's Task Force on the City University of New York.* Daniel Patrick Moynihan, *Miles to Go: A Personal History of Social Policy* (Cambridge, Mass.: Harvard University Press, 1996), p. 36.

40. Alan Wolfe, *One Nation, After All* (New York: Viking, 1998), pp. 166, 169.

41. Antonio Gramsci, *Selections from the Prison Notebooks,* ed. Quinton Hoare and Geoffrey Nowell Smith (New York: International Publishers, 1971), p. 324.

42. Melville, *Pierre,* pp. 258–259; Jill Ker Conway, *When Memory Speaks: Reflections on Autobiography* (New York: Knopf, 1998), pp. 15–16.

43. John Davenport, *The Saints Anchor-Hold in all Storms and Tempests* (London, 1682), p. 59.

44. John Dewey, *The Public and Its Problems* (1927; Chicago: Swallow Press, 1976), p. 142.

45. Tocqueville, *Democracy in America,* trans. Lawrence, pp. 296–297.

46. Streidt, quoted in Townsend Hoopes and Douglas Brinkley, *F.D.R. and the Creation of the U.N.* (New Haven: Yale University Press, 1997), p. 20. Christopher Lasch, quoted in Jean Bethke Elshtain, "On Christopher Lasch," *Salmagundi,* Spring–Summer 1995, 154.

47. Gombrowicsz, quoted in Alain Finkielkraut, *The Defeat of the Mind* (New York: Columbia University Press, 1995), p. 102.

48. Emerson, *Divinity School Address,* in Whicher, ed., *Selections from Emerson,* p. 115.

Index

Adams, Henry: *The Education of Henry Adams,* 84, 89
Addams, Jane, 91
Adorno, Theodor, 103–104
Alcoholics Anonymous, 24–26, 28, 43
Alger, Horatio, 74
Arendt, Hannah, 63
Arnold, Benedict, 53
Asimov, Isaac, 97

Bancroft, George, 132n46
Bell, Daniel, 88
Bellah, Robert, 94–95
Bennett, William, 84
Beverley, Robert: *The History and Present State of Virginia,* 40
blacks, rights of, 9–10, 67–72, 74, 76, 87–88
Bloom, Harold, 73
Bly, Robert, 102

Bok, Derek, 135–136n22
Bradford, William, 83
Brooks, Van Wyck, 33, 89
Brother Jonathan, 53
Brown, John, 74, 75
Brown v. Board of Education, 92
Brownson, Orestes, 58–59
Burr, Aaron, 53
Burton, Robert, 2
Bush administration, 93
Butler, Jon, 16
Byrd, William, 39–40

Calef, Robert, 38
Carnegie, Andrew, 90
Chambers, Robert, 50
Channing, William Ellery, 42
Chapman, John Jay, 90, 91
children, expectations of for the future, 98, 110–111
citizenship, 58, 93, 111

Index

City University of New York, 110
civil religion, 94–97, 111–112
Civil War, 7, 52, 71, 90, 91
Collingwood, R. G., 6
Compromise of 1850, 69
Constitution, U.S., 69, 73
consumer culture, 5, 103–105,
    107–111, 113, 115
Conway, Jill Ker, 113
Cotton, John, 22, 27, 32, 33, 34,
    37–38, 42, 83
Crane, Stephen, 21–22
Crockett, Davy, 53
culture, definitions of, 10, 23

Davenport, John, 33, 115
Declaration of Independence, 10,
    69, 73, 75
declension, 41–42
DeLillo, Don, 85
Democracy in America (Toc-
    queville), 2–3, 15, 18, 48, 51,
    53, 56, 60–61, 64–65, 67, 87,
    105, 107, 108–109, 116
Democratic Vistas (Whitman), 7,
    52, 54, 56, 91, 109
depression, 3–4, 98–101, 106,
    107
Dewey, John, 34, 115–116
Disney, 97–98
Douglass, Frederick, 69, 71; My
    Bondage and My Freedom, 72, 78
Dred Scott decision, 92, 72
DuBois, W. E. B., 9–10

Edwards, Jonathan, 22, 26, 33;
    Personal Narrative, 30–31; "Sin-
ners in the Hands of an Angry
    God," 21; A Treatise Concerning
    Religious Affections, 32, 35–
    36
Eliot, George, 51
Emancipation Proclamation, 9,
    71, 92
Emerson, Ralph Waldo, 34, 50,
    51–52, 54, 70, 84, 97; Divinity
    School Address, 43, 47–48, 51,
    59, 118; "Circles," 10; "Experi-
    ence," 4; Nature, 32
Enlightenment, 5, 42
equality, 58–59, 64, 78, 87–89,
    117–118
Europe, in contrast to American
    ideals, 48–49, 60–61, 66–67,
    79
expansion, westward, 57

Federalist Papers, 62–63
Finch, Francis Miles, 54
Franklin, Ben, 74
Freud, Sigmund, 29
future, views of, 9–10, 53, 86–
    87, 91–92, 110–111, 116–
    118; collapse of faith in, 96–98

Gates, Henry Louis, 86
gay rights, 93, 113–114
Geertz, Clifford, 1
Genesis, book of, 20, 22
George, Henry, 91
Gibson, William, 97
globalism, 115, 117–118
God, Puritan conception of, 19–
    22, 23–24, 26

Index

Gombrowicsz, Witold, 117
grace, Puritan conception of, 27–28, 32, 33
Gramsci, Antonio: *Prison Notebooks,* 112
Greene, Graham, 98

Hale, Edward Everett, 54
Hale, Nathan, 53
Hawthorne, Nathaniel, 56; *Blithedale Romance,* 89; "The Minister's Black Veil," 41, *Scarlet Letter,* 54
Hendrix, Jimi, 96
historiography, problems of, 6–10, 111
Hofstadter, Richard, 9
Hooker, Richard: *Of the Laws of Ecclesiastical Polity,* 18
Hooker, Thomas, 20, 28, 32, 103
hope, 1–6, 8, 10, 11, 16, 19, 27, 43, 67–68, 78, 86–87, 95–98, 103, 110–111, 116–118

immigration, 64, 88–89
individualism, 64, 103–106, 108–109, 117
Irving, Washington, 54

Jackson, Andrew, 96
James, Henry: *The Bostonians,* 89
James, William, 34; *Pragmatism,* 6; *The Varieties of Religious Experience,* 25–26, 28, 35, 53, 91–92

Jay, John, 62
Jefferson, Thomas, 10, 64, 73, 95–96, 107; *Notes on the State of Virginia,* 9, 61, 62, 63, 69
jeremiad, 83–87, 111
Johnson, Lyndon, 94
justification, Puritan view of, 22–23

Kallen, Horace, 88–89
Kansas-Nebraska Act, 70
Kirsch, Adam, 102–103

Lapham, Lewis, 104–105
Lasch, Christopher, 117
Lawrence, D. H., 18, 102
Lears, T. Jackson, 85
Leatherstocking, 53
Lemann, Nicholas, 133n2
Lewinsky, Monica, 135n21
Lincoln, Abraham, 70–80, 87–88, 90, 92, 108, 109, 118; *Address to the Wisconsin Agricultural Society,* 74; *Second Inaugural Address,* 77–78, 109; *Speech at Chicago, Illinois,* 79; *Speech at New Haven,* 74; *Speech on Dred Scott Decision,* 72; *Speech on Kansas-Nebraska Act,* 71, 77; *Speech on the Sub-Treasury at Springfield, Illinois,* 59
Lyell, Charles, 50

Macdonald, Dwight, 104
Madison, James, 62
Mailer, Norman: *The Armies of the Night,* 6

Index

Manifest Destiny, 57–59
Marion, Francis, 53
marketplace, pressures of: on Puritans, 31–33; on modern life, 90–91, 105–106, 115
Mather, Cotton, 38, 42; *Magnalia Christi Americana,* 23, 26, 38, 40
Mather, Increase, 38
melancholy, 2–4, 10, 11, 40, 70, 98, 106, 107, 112
Melville, Herman, 4, 55–58, 63, 68–69; *Moby-Dick,* 55–56, 60, 68; *Pierre,* 50, 112; *White-Jacket,* 57–58
Miller, Perry, 15–16, 41
Millerites, 50
Milton, John, 37
Missouri Compromise, 69
Moby-Dick (Melville), 55–56, 60, 68
Model of Christian Charity, A (Winthrop), 36
Mormons, 50
Moynihan, Daniel Patrick, 110
mythology, American, 53–54

nationalism as religion, rise of, 52–57, 59–60, 77–80
national literature, rise of, 53–56
nativism, 61–64
New Deal, 92
New York Times Magazine, 108
nostalgia, 83–85
Notes on the State of Virginia (Jefferson), 9, 61, 62, 63, 69
Noyes, John Humphrey, 50

Oakeshott, Michael, 4
O'Brien, Conor Cruise, 5

Paradise Lost (Milton), 36–37
Percy, Walker, 41, 99–102; *Love in the Ruins,* 99–101
Perkins, William, 30, 125n21
positivism, 7
postmodernism, 8, 98, 107
pragmatism, 8, 34–36
Progressivism, 92
Puritans, 17–43, 57, 96, 117
Putnam, Robert, 84, 133n2

race, American theories of, 58, 63, 64, 71, 76
Readings, Bill, 94
Reagan, Ronald, 96
Reconstruction, 87
Redford, Robert, 84
reform, social, 89–91, 96
rights, 64, 79, 87–89, 92–94, 117–118
Rockefeller, John D., 90, 134n13
Roosevelt, Franklin, 96, 98
Rorty, Richard, 34, 107

Sabbatarian movement, 49
Safire, William, 87
salvation, 22–23, 27–31, 33–34, 36, 43
Sargent, Epes, 54
Scarlet Letter, The (Hawthorne), 54
Schaff, Philip: *America,* 48, 49, 59, 61–62, 64
Schlesinger, Arthur M., Jr., 84

sects, religious, 17, 49–50, 114
self: Puritan view of, 22–31, 42–
    43, 117; modern view of, 103–
    110
sermons, Puritan, 27–31
service, social, 90–91
Sewall, Samuel, 39
sex, 102–103
Shepard, Thomas, 20–21
Sibbes, Richard, 25, 26
"Sinners in the Hands of an An-
    gry God" (Edwards), 21
slavery, 8–9, 64, 68–73
Song of Myself (Whitman), 55
statistics, 98, 106, 110, 135n22
Steffens, Lincoln, 91
Stephens, Alexander, 78
Strauss, David Friedrich: *Life of
    Jesus,* 50
Streidt, Clarence: *Union Now,* 117
symbols: Christian, 33, 56–57,
    59–60, 77; national, 53, 59–
    60, 77–78, 79–80, 92, 94–95

Taylor, Alan, 15
Thoreau, Henry David, 74–75; *A
    Plea for Captain John Brown,* 74–
    75; *Walden,* 78, 89
Tocqueville, Alexis de, 64–68,
    105–106, 113, 114; *Democracy
    in America,* 2–3, 15, 18, 48,
    51, 53, 56, 60–61, 64–65, 67,
    87, 105, 107, 108–109, 116
transcendence, 1–2, 5–6, 37, 59,
    78, 91–92, 94, 101–102, 114–
    115

*Treatise Concerning Religious Af-
    fections, A* (Edwards), 32, 35–
    36
Trilling, Lionel, 98
Trollope, Frances, 48–49
Twain, Mark, 4, 77

Uncle Sam, 53
utopianism, 53, 89–90, 92

Varieties of Religious Experience
    (James), 25–26, 28, 35, 53,
    91–92
Veblen, Thorstein: *The Theory of
    the Leisure Class,* 103
Vidal, Gore, 84
Vietnam war, 58, 94

Walden (Thoreau), 78, 89
Washington, George, 54
Weems, Mason Locke, 53
Wharton, Edith, 90
Whitman, Walt, 57; *Democratic
    Vistas,* 7, 52, 54, 56, 91, 109;
    Song of Myself, 55; *Specimen
    Days,* 95
Wigglesworth, Michael, 4, 77
Williams, William Carlos, 18
Wilson, Edmund, 73
Winthrop, John, 19, 20, 29, 38,
    96; *A Model of Christian Char-
    ity,* 36
Wolfe, Alan, 112
women's rights, 38, 48–49, 87,
    93
Woodstock, 96